"A heartwarming trip through the ruins of youthful delusion, much of which I don't remember."
Peter Capaldi

"Here we have the trampings of a slight Chaplinesque figure whose fickle fate seldom tires of tripping him up."
Finlay MacLeod

"The moors, a hamster perishing from hypothermia, the drinking habits of Glaswegian punks, the fascination with boxing, a sheep in a house, the outdoorsy tramping ... the subjects are indeed bleak. But the writing is animated, curious, precise and horribly candid. Not bleak. Nor are the many incidental digressions and the constant wryness. Invigorating as a gallon of Lanliq with an Eldorado chaser." **Jonathan Meades**

My parents and brothers, Carnival Day,
Stornoway, 1966. (I got lost.)

the mundane comedy

r. m. murray

Published by Saraband
Digital World Centre, 1 Lowry Plaza
The Quays, Salford, M50 3UB

www.saraband.net

ISBN: 9781912235605
ebook: 9781912235612

Printed and bound in Great Britain by Clays Ltd, Elcograf S.p.A.

1 3 5 7 9 10 8 6 4 2

*Names and various identifying details have been changed
in a number of places throughout this book.*

For Moira

Early mishap. Ness, Isle of Lewis, 1961

"The sense of unhappiness is so much easier to convey than that of happiness."

Graham Greene, *The End of the Affair*

Se am pian a tha nad' cheann fhein is miosa.
It's the pain in your own head that's worst.

Sean-fhacal / Gaelic proverb

"When you describe an experience, what you are recounting is your memory of the act, not the act itself. Experiencing a moment is an inarticulate act. There are no words. It is in the sensory world. To recall it and to put words to it is to illustrate how one remembers the past, rather than actually experiencing the past. Keep this in your mind as you read the words of others as they remember an incident."

Michael Winter, *All This Happened*

Contents

Part III: This Island Earth

Part IV: Leftovers

Part V: Swan Songs Unsung

Introduction

The published narratives of endurance are typically on a heroic scale. Of triumph over outsize adversity: exploration, adventure, enterprise. Life-threatening illness, or injury, abuse, addiction, deprivation, personal loss, man-made and natural disasters. Fanatical parents. How I was trapped, kidnapped, held hostage… War.

Or, how I framed my own DIY legend, by recreating a mythic "in the footsteps of" historical journey, or challenged myself to cross Australia on a unicycle.

The default celebrity memoir testifies to the emptiness and responsibility of fame, money, success and power. And the pilgrimage to redemption and fulfilment.

Yet because they represent the extremes and the extraordinary in human endeavour, they are by definition unrepresentative, non-relatable. They are XXL experiences. Not a good fit for the smaller figure. While our bespoke, bottled-up self-knowledge expands from within to occupy, shape or distend us.

At the time of writing, I've still got all my own teeth, never broken a bone, been in a car crash or spent a night in hospital. Never had an STD, not allergic to anything I know of, will eat most things put in front of me, never been abused, entered a court of law or even had points on my driving licence… It all points to a dearth of decent material, of character-forming drama. Technically, I'm ineligible.

And now the context has changed. It's all extreme. In the midst of a global pandemic we have lost our bearings and moorings. It's too big. Too unpredictable and unfathomable.

This testament, although it hasn't altered or moved since it was written, now sits in a different place. The mood has shifted.

The contrast control is malfunctioning, veering between horror and banality. From footage of mass graves to memes on domestic incarceration. Tragedy and toilet rolls.

"If I'm spared" – the grim, fate-laden qualifier to any statement of intent on the Isle of Lewis – I can now say without irony.

So. What to say? What to do? What else but soldier on. Read on. It is what it is and we are where we are.

To not identify or involve others – those who, out of necessity, choice, or a variant of luck, had some part to play in my life – I've had to smudge, compress, delete, shunt, feint, relocate, rename and lie a bit. That said, it's all true. Mostly.

R.M. Murray, July 2020

Part I

Growing Pains

'Island exports': The *Loch Seaforth* with herring barrels, 1960s.
*From the T B Macaulay Collection, by kind permission
of Mrs Kirsty Maciver.*

Cur-na-Mara

After the war, my father worked as the Collector of Dues for the Stornoway Pier and Harbour Commission. He met my mother in the ticket office at the ferry terminal for MacBrayne shipping company. Soon after, in 1955, they got married. I was born in 1956. Two years later, my brother Iain arrived, then Donald in 1960 and Kenneth Malcolm in 1964. It's how things were done.

At the time, the mainland connection with Stornoway was the railhead at Mallaig with a stop-over at Kyle of Lochalsh. The mail steamer that plied that route from 1947 to 1972 was the *Loch Seaforth*. And in all that time it only ever missed one sailing as a result of bad weather: the 31st of January, 1953, when the 7,000-tonne cargo liner *Clan MacQuarrie* ran aground at Borve on the west coast of Lewis, resulting in the largest 'breeches buoy' rescue in history.

Much was made of the barely imaginable ferocity of that storm. But it was the fact that even the *Loch Seaforth* had not sailed that night that emphatically put it into perspective.

As an adult, you are the sum total and resolution of all your mistakes. In time you might stand at the same vantage point your parents once did, recognise the place and experience a kind of retroactive empathy. As I have. Even so, I still find it baffling as to why they thought it a good idea to take four young children on a near twenty-four-hour round trip to Mallaig on the *Loch Seaforth*. They told us we were going on a cruise.

My youngest brother was still a baby, so I could only have been eight years old. The outward leg was overnight and, just before midnight, long past our bedtime, we got a lift into Stornoway and drew up outside the art deco ferry terminal on Number 1 Pier, boarding via the dimly lit, steep gangplank. The weather was not remarkable enough to recall.

With her graphic black, white and red livery, embellished with gold, the *Loch Seaforth* was the flagship of MacBrayne fleet. An impressive, imposing vessel, she embodied the stout values of pride, order and competence in the established tradition of British merchant shipping. Her handsome nautical trim an ensemble of wooden railings and decking, lifebelts and lifeboats, coiled ropes and fluttering flags.

On board, my parents talked and smoked with acquaintances in the haze of the saloon while we ran around and explored. There was an air of general conviviality and anticipation. A chatter and hum. Soon after casting off, we were taken down to our quarters towards the bow on the starboard side.

It was not spacious. Or comfortable. The mattresses were unyielding and covered in a bristly, stippled material while the ground tone was the thundering thrum and smell of the engines, counterpointed by the pervasive aftertaste of the galley. None of which mattered in the broader context of this huge adventure.

As we cleared the harbour and arced our way out to sea, the initially benign motion of the ship gradually matured into a slow, metronomic swing. The ominous development reaching its optimum when the porthole above our berths began to submerge under a green and white froth and then yaw up to the night sky as a recurrent black hole.

Bottled in our cabin, we watched this hypnotic ballet as excitement fought exhaustion and an encroaching queasiness, until exhaustion and oblivion prevailed.

And morning arrived. At around 6am we entered Loch Alsh and approached Kyle in a pale grey, smudged drizzle. Dense, low cloud cropped the surrounding mountains. The vessel was stable and although sleep had quelled the nausea I had incubated during

the night, it had not dispelled it. I had no appetite for a full breakfast of porridge, bacon and eggs, or even tea and toast.

Out on deck, there was activity. Crew members paced, shouted
and flung ropes as the ship manoeuvred and docked. We were on
the mainland. And the thrill of exploring Kyle, if only for an hour
or so, was restorative. Fuelled by our imagination, my brother Iain
and I raced down the gangplank and along the pier. The main
road turned to the right along the seafront but straight ahead it
rose. We set out to crest the low hill and explore the town hinterland, only to find, two minutes later, that there was nothing
beyond that point but mountain and moor. We had plenty of that
at home. It was an early lesson in expectation management.

A couple of hours later, we were in Mallaig in the rain and
spent some time in a chandlery, looking at fishing lures, gamely
maintaining the sense of adventure and novelty. We had tea and
scones in a nearby hotel. By now I had learned that Stornoway was
a huge town. Another lesson: appreciate what you have.

Still, I felt better. Soon be home. In fact, we were only halfway.

The sheltered waters and relative calm between Kyle and
Mallaig banished the half-memory of the overnight crossing,
and as we made our passage back up the Sound of Sleat we sat in
the dining room as a family for high tea. The setting aspired to a
floating Grand Hotel: a small-scale, budget version of the imperial aesthetic of the great ocean liners. We were formally attired
for public viewing in shirts, ties, V-neck pullovers, school blazers, short trousers and knee-high socks, with polished shoes and
combed hair. My parents, a snapshot in Sunday best.

The serving staff in aprons and white tunics brought fried chops,
liver and onions, steak pie, mashed potatoes, boiled vegetables,
side dishes, bread rolls, pudding and custard in lavish portions.
As if it was intended as personal ballast. Emblematic amid the
colossal spread was a jaundice-yellow pickled cauliflower floret.

Growing boys, we ate heartily, and as we finished our meal the *Loch Seaforth* headed out of Loch Alsh and into the open waters of the Minch and the final leg of our cruise.

And then, a suggestion of motion. A saucer slid tentatively towards me. I pushed it back but it came at me again. More assertively. More aggressively. Soon the condiments, cutlery and crockery began to skid and skim across the counters and table tops in choreographed chaos, and the serving staff began to collect all loose items from each surface. The room swayed. The horizon dipped. The ship began to climb and plunge at ever more improbable and alarming gradients. She rose and fell, fell and rose, rolled and rolled.

The wind whipped plumes of spray and spume across the decks and lathered the windows. The sea was a sullen, angry, colourless grey, streaked with white. Horizon blended into sky. Passengers who stood up became silent-movie comedy drunks ridiculously compensating for each lurch, slew and stagger as they slalomed through the tables. The crew waltzed on, collecting ashtrays.

Intensified by the suffocating heat, the smell of diesel, galley and cigarettes now infected everything. In no time, it had become oppressive, overpowering, unbearable. And there could be no escape, respite or sanctuary in the cradle of sleep or the bosom of the Sound of Sleat. Iain and Donald looked and felt like I did. Pale, clammy, unhappy. We'd stopped talking.

My father took charge, led us outside, and we emerged into a shockingly cold, violently windy brine-wash. A saline slap in the face. But still the better of the two hopeless options available: inside or on deck.

Now sickness broke inside me like a malignant egg. My stomach tensed, tightened, began to spasm, and I blurted out my first instalment of vomit, at pressure, downwind. And again. And again. And yet again.

It became an uncontrollable, autonomous function, like your heartbeat or metabolism. Helplessly, I watched as a viscous eruption, cobwebbed by the wind into a long spiralling ribbon, whirled past a startled passenger who had emerged on deck. An ethereal, graceful thing, it flecked the shoulder of his mackintosh before it atomised and vanished in the haze.

Time telescoped, misery condensed and distilled. The universe collapsed, concentrated, foamed and churned in the crucible of my being. I retched until there could surely not be a thimbleful of nutrient contaminant left. And still it kept coming. Heaving, hoiking, gagging, my viscera a clenched fist, until there were only dry cramping contractions. Crushed with exhaustion, my ribcage vacuum-packed by the relentless, unstoppable internal effort.

Only if Hell was a worse version of what I was going through did I want to stay alive. But what could be worse than this?

Pitilessly, mercilessly, it went on. Five hours, six hours. What did it matter? It was incurable. I didn't even have the energy to care when there came a perceptible lessening in extremity and severity as we neared and took shelter in the leeway of Lewis.

The gyroscopes began to rebalance. Equilibrium and stability slowly returned. The transit was now exclusively forward. Enough to tip the balance of choice from the wretchedness, shivering cold and saturation of the passenger deck in favour of the stifling warmth and disgusting ambient flavour of the saloon. Where my mother was breastfeeding.

And we docked. And it was over. I had survived. Yet, on the pier, I lurched, teetered and staggered as the ground angled and tipped, lifted and dropped. I skewed my way to the waiting car while the earth itself stood still. The sea within me.

Crammed into the back of an Austin A30 with my mother and three brothers, convalescence could begin and the ordinary and mundane re-established during the seven-mile drive home. I only remember an overwhelming vacant tiredness. Later that night, I was astounded to find that I was starving and was offered a sausage roll. But I just couldn't do it.

As a life experience it was formative. A rite of passage, indeed. But later, in a peculiar sense, I came to regard it more as an inoculation: where a tincture or derivative of a disease is introduced into the body as a means of developing a resistance to it. And this only because I have not been seasick since.

The Hook

"Fishing is a delusion entirely surrounded by liars in old clothes."

Don Marquis

Fishing was as much a religion as it was the defining recreation of my youth. A moral, philosophical value system. There were disciplines and processes, rites, rituals, mythologies.

The River Coll at the bottom of our croft still had salmon until they were wiped out by netting. And there were rock-fishing stations all along the coast with resonant names, now forgotten. Rubha nan Gall (The Headland of Strangers), Creag na Saille (The Fat Rock), Na Pollan Gorm (The Blue-Green Pools), Slighe-Brìghe (Drift-path), Caiptean Làthair (the Captain's Place), Gob an Rubha (the Beak of the Headland)…

My father was interested exclusively in trout and salmon fishing. He would go down to the Coll or Gress rivers each night after work, or fish for sea trout with a spinning rod from the beach at the estuary. He went on expeditions to some of the innumerable lochs that colandered the wilderness of the Ness and Barvas Moors. Or, on occasion, would get a permit to a salmon loch on the Creed system, or Loch Langabhat, at seven miles long the largest body of water on the island. Anything outside the district was restricted and rationed by transport requirements. Cars were scarce.

In time, we got to accompany him on these expeditions. Shorter trips at first, but increasingly on more ambitious forays. I suppose he couldn't get out of it. Maybe he accepted that we were an unavoidable handicap, the going rate to prosecute his passion.

All the lochs could be categorised. As if they had a personality. Moody or fresh, frivolous or deep, serious… It could be based on remoteness and accessibility; the profusion, type and size of trout; the clearness of the water; whether it had steep banks, deep pools or shelving beaches. Whether it was exposed or sheltered. And so on. Some lochs were rarefied. A stiff loch meant that fish were few and far between. Shy, unaccommodating, reluctant or too clever to be caught. But if you did catch one, it was almost certain to be huge. Loch Sgeireach na Creaga Briste (the Loch on the Cliff of Broken Rock), on the Ness–Tolsta moor, was an excellent example. You might sit there all day in perfect conditions and see nothing. As we used to say, you only needed one worm for the whole day. You might leave convinced that there were, in fact, no fish at all under that dead water. But you'd go back. And the same thing would happen again.

These lochs denied and defied you. Challenged your skill, your patience, your character. Going there was a commitment of serious intent. A virility test.

Loch an as Sgeil, on the Barvas Moor, was another such loch. Rigid, resistant and miles away. And we were going there, so the preparations began.

The night before was for digging worms. Typically, these were kept in a Golden Virginia tobacco tin that had a few holes punched into the lid. Then getting the rods ready. Spare line, bubble floats and hooks. For this loch, lead weights were the order of the day. All the other stuff – sandwiches, biscuits, a tin of condensed milk, flask of tea – was what my mother did. And it was always an early start.

My brother Iain and I were to be joined by Alec, who lived across the road. He was a few years older than us. Not academic. He couldn't string a sentence together without saying "all the time". Which he said all the time. Even if we were speaking

Gaelic. Latterly, all he ever did was sit at his window watching the intermittent traffic. But he did have abilities. Forty years on, he could remember the number plates of cars and vans that had passed through the village, all the way back to the Sixties. It was as obvious to him as reading it off a card. Nor could he understand how this was remarkable. "That's just the number," he would say. Perplexed as to why you might doubt him.

We set off at about seven o'clock in the morning. It was an overcast day with intermittent sunshine and a light westerly breeze. No rain, midges or wind from the north or east. Good conditions. Propitious.

Loch an as Sgeil was a long walk. Longer for an eight-year-old. A car would have knocked a mile off it, but we didn't have that option. Out the tarmac single track road for half a mile and then the peat road for a further mile up the Coll river, past the striations of village peat banks and, finally, the open moor.

In the *World at War* episode about the German invasion of the Soviet Union, narrator Sir Laurence Olivier describes the demoralising effect on the German troops as they become like ants in the endless, flat, featureless landscape of the Russian Steppes, with its eternal horizon. It resonated. I knew that state of mind from fishing expeditions like this. The moor stretched ahead as if we were doomed to walk it forever. Our destination unreachable, held at a continuous, consistent distance by the pressure wave of our expectation.

The terrain varied: knee-high heather, *mòinteach bhriste* (broken moorland), sucking bog, springy turf, long stretches that were like walking on a wet mattress.

But there was an electric thrill to that first glimpse of the loch reflecting the sky in a distant dip. A shot of adrenalin. Suddenly, there was hope. Suddenly, there was a point to all this. We were nearly there. Only we weren't. The trudge had to continue for another half hour.

On the steep banks of the lochside, there was a frantic fumbling and urgency to get the rods out. As if we only had ten minutes and not ten hours to sit and fish this dusky lapping water. Miles from anywhere with only windsong and birdsong.

My dad helped thread the nylon line through the rings of my split cane rod, and we tied on the lead weights and skewered the sacrificial worms onto the hook. The same for Iain, and a bit of help for Alec.

There's a sacred space between the infinite and the particular. It lies in these preoccupied, concentrated moments under the enormous canopy of the sky, trying to push a barely visible eight-pound breaking-strain nylon line through the microdot eye of a fish hook. Like darning a sock in a vast open field, oblivious to the universe.

What would now happen is that the three rods would be cast and my father would leave us where we were and make his way round the bank, whipping the water with his fly rod, or spinning a Mepps, covering every inch of loch. Doing what he loved doing. Serious focused fishing on a rare, blessed day off, while we sat by ourselves for hours. Taken care of. We would check the worms from time to time, get bored, mess about, tell stories, eat biscuits, catch glimpses of him on the far side of the loch and perhaps see him again in the early afternoon after he had completed a circuit. He might even have caught something.

That was the script.

What happened was that Alec took his rod, swung it back to cast and slammed the hook, worm and all, into the crook of my leg. Right behind my knee. It went in all the way, past the barb up to the shank. I buckled. It was like being punched and punctured at the same time. Only a doctor was going to fix this.

As a fishing trip, the whole day was now finished. Wrecked.

Kaput. We had spent well over two hours walking to the loch and been there five minutes. Now, not only did we have to pack up and head straight back, my dad would have to carry me all the way.

I can only imagine what he thought. What he felt. Concern? Despair? Frustration? Fury? That this was some kind of cosmic joke? Probably a potent cocktail of all of these. Perhaps he wanted to throw Alec into the loch. I can't say. I could say, at least, that it wasn't my fault.

I didn't know and didn't want to know how they were going to get the hook out. But that was a problem that lay miles and hours ahead. We packed up everything and I was hoisted onto my father's back while rods and rucksacks were redistributed between Iain and Alec.

The trek back was of a different emotional hue. Instead of anticipation and optimism, there was resignation, defeat. It wasn't just another failed, fishless expedition; we hadn't even had the chance to fail. So it felt longer and took longer. Longer squared. For my poor father in his role as pack pony, it must have been a gruelling, dispiriting slog. Still, these guys had been in the war.

Our party staggered home in the early afternoon. As usual, my mother and Auntie Peggy were talking and drinking tea by the window in the living room. Probably their eleventh cup of the day. Once the consternation and alarm had subsided, a car was procured and we got a lift to the doctor in Stornoway. In the surgery, I was rested on my belly over a wooden laboratory stool and, with a pair of pliers – and without anaesthetic – the brusque medic forced the hook deeper, so that the point and the barb curved back out and through my skin. Then he snapped the tip off with wire cutters and pulled the rest of the shaft back through.

It was, of course, painful. I never saw what it looked like, but I imagine with the entry and the exit so close together that it was like a vampire bite.

Because of the nature of the lesion, in that it had an earthworm and a plenitude of microbial life on it, he applied a hot poultice. And for days, this was regularly changed, re-applied and bandaged. I remember my mother boiling it up in the scullery on the electric cooker.

Walking and Falling

I'm still primary-school age when my father takes us fishing to Loch Sgiobacleit in South Lochs, my two brothers and our friend Callum. It's a decent salmon loch. A vast T-shaped body of water at the top of the Seaforth Head river system. Too big and distant to be effectively policed by the Eishken estate, who own the fishing rights.

After a long winding drive in our MG Magnette, we park in a small, disused quarry and traverse a low rise and a lumpy mile of moor down to the loch. There, brimful with anticipation, we set our rods, after which my father leaves us to make his own way with a fly rod around the lochside. Casting in a fan pattern, wafting the silk line and tiny feathers over the dark, wrinkled water. Eventually, he disappears from sight.

Emptiness. Silence. Not a living thing to be seen except two eagles wheeling overhead on the edge of the stratosphere. Time suspended.

Hours later, nothing has happened and when he reappears we tell him that we are going to try Loch na Ciste, a reliable trout loch over the ridge. But he isn't giving up on the prospect of catching a salmon and says he'll see us later. Probably glad to be rid of us for a while. So we pack up, climb the hill and begin again at the smaller loch. Where, in due course, we catch some small trout.

The afternoon wears on. Imperceptibly, the light fades. It is late summer, coming into September and the long days have contracted. Afternoon segues into evening. Evening begins to deepen into night. Unseen, a snipe drums overhead. It's time to go.

But where? Maybe Dad has gone straight back to the car and assumed that we will do the same of our own accord. Or maybe he's waiting for us at the other loch. He said he'd see us later. We take the latter option. Only, by the time we are halfway there, in the gathering night, do we realise that the only course of action is to head for the car. We have a rough idea of the direction.

Now it is pitch dark. We can't see our feet or the ground. We walk two steps, randomly fall on our faces; another step, smack down; two steps, three steps, a lateral lurch into a hole-in-the-moor; we fall and drag ourselves up, collapse and fall some more, again and again. It's relentless. In the black, an aural slapstick of thumps, gasps, winded sighs, the slap and suck of wellies, the abrasive, scrubby brush of heather.

An accumulating panic.

Then the horizon is revealed by an aura. A car's headlamps. And, on the thin wind, we can hear Dad shouting desperately at the top of his voice. We shout back. And again. A shrill chorus. Our helpless choreography continues. We keep shouting, walking, falling, walking, shouting, falling. Smashing into the ground. Getting up. Battered by the earth.

When we crest the ridge, an illuminated knobbly pathway opens up before us with my father silhouetted dramatically against the headlights, his shadow stretching out as he strides, now runs, to meet us.

This Big

I was fifteen when we went on holiday for the first time. My parents rented a house in Inverasdale on Loch Ewe on the west coast. It's a deep sea loch. There was a naval station at Aultbea, on the other side.

Most days, my father hired a small boat with an outboard motor for sea fishing. We used a *dorgh* (a handline) to catch pollock, saithe, cod, haddock. Sometimes mackerel.

This time, I baited the two haddie hooks on the trace, dropped the lead weight over the side and unspooled the interminable brown cord until there was no length left. We drifted. And then a distant thump and a slow pull on the line. I yanked back to ensure the hook embedded, and prepared to reel in.

Unlike a rod where you "play" a fish till it's exhausted, on a *dorgh* it's just a long haul, hand-over-hand, into the boat. I'd caught decent-sized fish often enough and had a good predictive sense of their eventual size from the weight and struggle through the line: a neural transmission from the bottom of the sea. On this occasion, the line was singing with tension. It rasped on the gunnel of the boat and thrummed in the water. I couldn't even hold it, far less pull it in. And, as my father furiously ordered me to "keep the strain", suddenly it went slack. Confusingly, I felt both crestfallen and relieved as I began the long process of reeling in. When the heavy nylon trace finally came back into the boat, I saw that the hook had been pulled straight.

Most likely, it had been a barndoor skate. If so, it could have weighed over 200 pounds. Its wingspan as wide as our boat.

30% by Volume

Introducing a Gaelic poem called *An Turas* ("The Journey") at a reading in the late Eighties, the writer Ruaraidh MacThòmais (Derick Thomson) said that it was about someone with a debilitating condition. And so rife throughout the *Gàidhealtachd* that it was all the more remarkable that there wasn't even a Gaelic word for it: "alcoholic".

He was right and he was wrong. There were no alcoholics. Slang and euphemism swathed the word in an insulating blanket, so there were only those who were *trom air an deoch* (heavy on the drink). Someone could be *air a dhalladh* (blind drunk) or *gun fuarachach* (never cooling down / ever over-heating). Or *tha e donn* (a reference to the ruddy brown face colour of the heavy user). And it was hard to afford a habit.

Most Lewis villages seemed about 30% by volume.

My Uncle Morris, who had been "hospitalised in Inverness following many years of alcoholic drinking", was a founding member of AA in Stornoway in the late Fifties and early Sixties. He wrote about an "abortive attempt in '53/'54" and his pessimism about the prospects that it might ever take root, because "I was under the delusion that Stornoway was different. AA might flourish in other places, but Stornoway with its narrow social outlook, tradition of religious intolerance, coupled with reputation for alcoholic excess would deride, misrepresent and kill our efforts with public cynicism. Events have proved me completely wrong."

Before then, the only official exit was through the church. It was a binary system. Swapping one type of community for another. One heavy drinker who had straightened himself out, single-handed, said he felt good but lamented his loss of society, that it was a lonely life.

Drinking culture was defined and contained by several factors. It was session-based. Social. Usually all-or-nothing weekend binges. Nobody had much money, so when it ran out, that tended to be it. It was hard drinking of hard liquor from a limited gantry. Almost exclusively whisky or dark (Trawler) rum. Pale ale, heavy and lager was "belly-wash". A nip and a half-pint chaser was the default order at the bar.

Access and availability influenced drinking patterns. There were no pubs or hotels in the villages. Coll, being seven miles from Stornoway, was a fair traipse away and bus-reliant. Hardly anybody had a car. The far-flung parish of Ness had *bothans**, a kind of socialism, or mutual society, or collective, where "members" paid a fixed amount and kegs of beer and assorted liquor were bought wholesale and consumed – like the NHS, free at the point of use – in the convivial surroundings of a bothy somewhere on the moor or machair, usually at a respectable distance from housing.

Sunday brought everything to a standstill. All the pubs, hotel bars, off-licences and shops were closed. No buses ran. If you had enough foresight you might have bought a carry-out the night before, with enough to tide you over. Anyway, there was hell to pay: church the following morning and evening. A duty and a penance.

Women did not drink. The wives, sisters, mothers and daughters who tried to keep things together. The hoops round the barrel. There were no female toilets in the bars. I never saw women drink much more than a sherry at New Year, or a snowball at a wedding or a half of lager in a hotel lounge bar.

Drinking was an entirely male pursuit. Everybody worked. Hard. On fishing boats. In the Harris Tweed mills. On the croft. In a sense, they were heroic figures. They deserved it. Ex-war. One, in fact, was called The Warrior.

Another, Zig-Zag, had been on the Russian convoys. Latterly, through age and rheumatism, his legs gave out and he would frequently be on all fours. Mostly, he'd been kept in line by his wife but after she died the shackles were off. No limits. Beware your freedom. After that, my mother would see him from our scullery window having come off the late bus, hanging on to a strainer or the gatepost, paralysed, unable to move. Wearily, she'd go over and help him into the house. One night, weeping after a routine rescue, he told her, "You know this, Ishbel? I'd give anything to have Maggy sitting in that chair across from me right now. Giving me hell."

Along the road, Small had been "at the whalers" in the Fifties in South Georgia. He was a special case even among the most battle-hardened boozers. His capacity limitless, his thirst unquenchable. Always an early starter, he'd wait for the bus in our porch while we got ready for school, shaking, shivering, quivering: in dire need of a livener.

At the whaling, they made hooch from any salvaged organic waste they could find, including driftwood, and always gave him the first bottle, which he would plank under his mattress. His need being greater. It was, by all accounts, the most undrinkable beverage ever created. But you always had a choice: take it or leave it.

One morning, after uncorking a batch in the shed where it had been distilled and stashed, they woke in their huts after the blowout and noticed that Small hadn't made it back. Outside, it was sub-zero so a search party was dispatched to recover the body. They found him covered by a light blanket of snow. He was fine.

Uncle Calum Iain was at the beginning of one of his dry spells. He had run out of the physical ability to resurrect himself from his daily overdoses and retreated to the cupboard that served as his bedroom under the eaves of our house. It had a skylight and was big enough for a single bed with a foot or so to spare on one side. Nothing else. There wasn't even room for a side table. In this sweat-lodge he marinated for days with a towel wrapped around his neck. An incarceration that made my father marvel at his prodigious bladder. Occasionally, we would poke our heads in to snicker or torture him. Or just to check that he was still alive.

Until his suffering got too much. Overwhelmed him. He said that he had planked a half-bottle of rum behind a chicken shed in the village and begged us to go and get it. When it was retrieved it was excellent entertainment denying him the bottle until eventually, bored with this theatre of cruelty, we handed it to him. He snatched it and stashed it under his bed. But never touched it. He just needed to know that it was there. He never drank again.

* From the 1976 supplement to the Scottish National Dictionary (1700–):

BOTHAN, n. An unlicensed drinking house or hut of dubious legality, esp. in the Island of Lewis, a kind of shebeen (see quot.) (Hebr. 1975). ['bɔθən; Gael. 'bɔhan]. w.Sc. 1963 Press & Jnl. (1 April): -

Altogether, there are about ten bothans in Ness and there are two at Shawbost. Some of them came into being about thirty years ago. The only licensed premises in Lewis are at Stornoway. The bothans – or shebeens – are normally situated on common pasture away from other houses in the village. No money is supposed to be transacted for the refreshments as each member is supposed to be a share-holder of the beer and whisky of the premises.

[Gael. *bothan*, id., a hut, shack.]

The Strap

Primary

On our first day at school, we were given a slate to write on. And a *sleipean* (slate-pen), which was a graphite stick to scratch onto the surface. It was a kind of Stone Age tablet that prefigured the touch-screen age.

The teacher – a severe, scraped-hair, elderly woman – went round each one and wrote down our first ever lesson. A maths problem: I + I. I hadn't a clue as to what this meant, or what to do, so I wrote 'II'. In Latin, it would have been correct. My maths didn't improve much over the years.

Later that week, I witnessed corporal punishment being administered for the first time. A boy, who was not keeping up, getting a thin leather strap smacked across his hand. And crying. In these first years, a ruler across the knuckles was a popular variant. Nothing too drastic.

In later life, the slate acquired a different significance. Seasoned drunks, if reliable enough, had a notional "slate" behind the bar. A credit system. There was an example of vernacular concrete poetry propped up behind the bar in the County Hotel: a slate with the word "NO" chalked on it. Art is everywhere.

Famously, a regular known in his heyday as Captain Blood, when out of cash, once threatened the barman that if he were not given more booze, he would take away his slate.

This was the soil, the loam, the environment in which attitudes grew and flourished. In films, TV and books there was sanitised, theatrical violence. While in homes and at official level in the classroom there was real *discipline*. And much else besides.

The Strap

By Primary Four, when we all – teachers and pupils – followed behind a piper along the road and up the hill from the Old School (long since demolished) to the modern New School, we took it all with us.

Case study: a couple of years hence. There was a new rule, for whatever reason, that pupils weren't allowed in the corridor at lunchtime. It wasn't strictly adhered to and neither teachers nor kids seemed to bother much about it. Which may be why one day we were caught engaged in some harmless horseplay in this demilitarised zone. Not by a teacher but by an apprentice Presbyterian saint called Mairi Joan, who was surely destined one day to become a minister's wife. She regularly won first prize in Bible and, as the perfect prefect, it was her sacred duty to report us.

There were four of us. And we were unaware of what was to befall us until the early afternoon when we were called out of class and summoned to Topdog's room to answer for it. He was a secondary school teacher on a temporary placement at the school.

We knocked and, on command, were given entry through the side door to an empty, chalky, light-bleached classroom. Evidently, he didn't have any classes that afternoon. Blackboard, plywood desks and chairs, a bit echoey. Sun behind the half-drawn blinds.

Topdog was ex-military, as most male teachers were at that time. Through duty: if not the war, National Service. And it was in that tradition that he addressed us formally by our surnames.

We stood to the side as he sat at his desk and shunted his chair round to confront us. Graphically silhouetted against the window, the light along his lean jaw and cheekbone revealed a pock-marked complexion. He had a high, polished forehead with dark hair combed back in the last vestiges of a widow's peak. It was a warm day but he was wearing his tweed jacket. Though he remained seated, he was still taller than us.

"Well, well, well…" he said slowly, sorrowfully, in a deep voice. "What have we to say for ourselves?" He had a Lewis accent, but the conversational tone and language was imperious, correct and formal.

I began to speak. Blurted out some kind of alibi or justification of why I had only been there by accident or coercion. Get in early. He wouldn't even know the circumstances. But even as I spoke, he opened a drawer and took out a thick, stiff, dark brown leather strap, which he let clatter onto his desk. A couple of feet long and bifurcated along a third of its length into two tongues, it curled on its side, unwinding menacingly like a waking serpent.

He let me babble on and looked at me mournfully. "That's a very sad story, Murray," he said, "very sad indeed. And I'm sure your mother would have her heart melted by it. I do believe she would. I do. But alas, Murray," he continued, shaking his head slowly and with an expression of helpless regret, "I do not have a heart. I have a stone."

In that moment, we all must have known we were done for. Nobody else was going to say anything from now on. Just so long as it was over quickly.

But something about the leisurely, recreational pace of this seminar suggested that might not be the case. There was an indefinable sense that, for Topdog, the prospect had brightened an otherwise routine, drab afternoon.

He turned his attention to the strap and began to describe and expound upon it in affectionate and imaginative detail. And with a grand vocabulary. "Look at it," he said. "Observe the remarkable thickness and robustness of that hide. What an extraordinary beast it must have come from. What do you suppose? A rhinoceros from the shores of Madagascar?"

We'd heard that his party trick was to put a piece of chalk on the desk and pulverise it with a single, vicious, descending lash. But this gathering did not require such a theatrical display. A demonstration of absolute force and the psychology of deterrence would not be necessary. It was too late for that.

So the solemn meditation on the origins, the function, the properties, the history of the strap continued. He invited us to dwell objectively, forensically and philosophically on it, as if it were a specimen in a lab, or a weapon recovered from the scene of a crime.

"Notice," he said, "how the ends are worn smooth and black?" We did. We were by now morbidly familiar with this weapon of extreme education. "That polished patina was acquired by all the years thrashing multiples of thugs during my time in Glasgow."

"I call it Excalibur," he revealed. "Do you know why that is?" I did. "It's the name of King Arthur's sword." He nodded with approval. "Indeed so." But even as the discourse turned to courage, chivalry, nobility and sacrifice, I knew it wasn't going to help me any.

By now, I felt like begging him to just do it. Get it over with. And in overdue course, as by now we must have missed a sizeable chunk of the afternoon, he obliged. We lined up, presented our crossed hands, palm up, for the first of two whipped, scorching lashes. Change hands. Repeat.

Until then, it had all seemed, if menacing, almost chummy. It did not even seem appropriate when it finally cracked into violence. It was a *non sequitur*. But there was a sense, too, that for him it was simultaneously duty and reward.

We walked back to our classroom, our hands hot, red, swollen mittens. But I suppose we also felt slightly heroic. The relief it was over, a kind of balm on our palms.

Many years later, as an adult, I attended an evening meeting at the same school and found myself wandering down the corridor where, all that time ago, we had transgressed. I looked into the darkened classroom and saw all the miniature chairs and desks. And, like little ghosts, I saw the four of us as very small boys with a slightly bewildered look on our faces, standing up and filing our way towards our fate.

And I wondered where the break in tradition had occurred that outlawed such ferocious retribution on young children. It was barely imaginable. Or was I just soft?

Secondary

Monday morning, first thing. A routine, rainy, winter's day, a gaggle of blazered fourteen-year-old girls and boys, chattering, squabbling, horsing about outside the school huts. Just after RE (Religious Education) and registration.

Next up is French, the first period of the day. Did you do your homework? No. I forgot. Did you? No. Everybody had forgotten about it. Or chosen not to do it. Or just not bothered. So, never mind, doesn't matter, safety in numbers. It wasn't a big deal.

Our French teacher was, of course, known to us as The Frog. A compact, dark, curly-haired, bushy-eyed, intense, animated, sometimes funny and mischievous character. He was also hard to read, unpredictable. Which made him scary. Sometimes, kids seemed to get away with heinous crimes: chewing gum in class, not paying attention, even not doing their homework. He might wag his finger. Tell you to spit it out into the waste-paper basket. Give you a hard stare. Warn against complacency. But there were other times...

Like that Friday afternoon we all waited in the corridor outside his room for the other class to come out. The bell had gone but the door remained shut. We sat on radiators and windowsills as the teaching time passed. Increasingly bemused, distracted, restless, speculating as to what was happening.

Eventually, the door opened and the previous class filed out silently, subdued, heads bowed, and quickly disappeared down the corridor. We went in. The Frog sat at his desk silent, motion-less, as we took our places.

Once settled, he said, "How many of you have seen this?" and waved the morning absentee sheet in the air. This was the regular daily bulletin that recorded anyone Missing In Action and any relevant or germane information for the coming school day. We all must have seen it or had it read out to us, but nothing remotely interesting or memorable ever appeared on that sheet. And today was no exception. So no one spoke. Which seemed like the wrong answer. The atmosphere was already inexplicably foreboding and charged, and no one knew why. It must have had something to do with the last class.

It was the end of the day and the end of the week. Afterwards, from four o'clock onwards was "Activities". This was a wide range of recreational, sporting, cultural, improving classes you could sign up to, from Archery to Bachelor Cooking, from Canoeing to Chess, Darts to Embroidery, all the way down the alphabet. You would have listed your first, second and third choice a couple of weeks ago. Then, in due course, turn up for Marquetry or Orienteering or Wood Carving.

He read out from the sheet: "All those who have not yet been allocated to an Activity must report to the rector at lunchtime." And with that he stood up and paced in front of us with a meas-ured tread. And repeated it. Solemnly, incredulously. Like an incantation. Amazed, it seemed, by what he was actually saying.

And then, just in case we had failed to understand the signif-icance of the sentence, he took it apart and laid it out in front of us. Explained. Apparently, from what I could gather, it should have read, "All those who have not had *an activity allocated to them*". The other way round. I suppose there was a difference but it seemed interchangeable. It was hard to see what this had to do with anything.

Even as we struggled to process this, it became evident that the situation could not be contained. It flashed over. What followed next was a condensed, outraged discourse that consumed any semantic argument, like a burning building incinerating the match that lit the fire. Within minutes, we were in occupied France during the Second World War: the oppression and coercion of civilians under the Nazis; the cattle trucks to the concentration camps; collaborators; the brutal violation of women. Murder. The Death Camps.

The absentee sheet, it seemed, was the thin end of the wedge.

The subliminal memory of that tirade stayed with me longer than anything I was ever taught about French verbs, and it would have been latent inside me as we sat for the first period on that Monday morning.

He seemed in a good mood. To be fair, he usually was. Good morning, chit chat and so forth. Then he asked one of the boys for his homework. Deep pause. He hadn't done it. So he asked the boy beside him. No, sir. Then he went round every pupil in the class – there must have been over thirty of us – and asked each one of us if we had done our homework. No, sir. No, sir... Not one of us. Not the boys. Not the girls.

Now the air became dense with a gathering silence. Until finally broken, quite lightly, almost casually with a shrug, when he said, "Very well. So. I shall give you the same choice I always do. You may have the belt or an imposition."

There were times when you might expect strict discipline. Other times you felt you might even deserve it. But first thing on Monday morning? We hadn't even woken up, got warmed up. And for this?

Dilemmas. Should I just get it over with? Short sharp shock. Could I face it this early? No. Lines might be better. Boring, tedious, mechanical. A chore, to be sure. But still. Hang on, though, this was French we were talking about. Could I bear *that*?

It's hard to say how the options were playing out with each individual and what the split of choices might be between the brave and the pragmatic when he suddenly declared, "I have changed my mind." Massive relief. The atmosphere lifted. It had just been a warning shot. To wake us up, shake us up. Get our attention.

"I have decided that I will belt all the boys and that the girls will have a choice."

So all the girls opted for the imposition. Lines. While the boys lined up in alphabetical order along the window wall for our two cross-hands. Bar maybe a Campbell, almost everybody's surname began with Mac so one of the first in line was Allan Macaskill, who had an arm in plaster at the time and could only hold up his unbroken limb to be lashed. Then the Macdonalds, Mackenzies, Macleods and so on. As a Murray, I was last in the queue. So I had all that time to watch his face as he administered each stroke. The concentration, the grimacing, accumulating anger, frightening and bewildering. With each lash, it seemed to escalate. With every pupil, every stroke, like some Doomsday clock, it notched nearer my turn.

There's a saying in chess – which I did for an Activity – that the threat is stronger than the execution. By the time I stood on my own in front of him, the threat had become a looming terror. I felt engulfed by it all. Dwarfed by this furious little man.

It was a companion piece to the primary school flaying. But this time, standing in line, it was less the psychology, more the chronology of it. Like you know that death is inevitable, but somehow, subliminally, believe that you are the exception.

Here, in miniature, in this functional civic theatre, on this wet Monday morning, I was confronted starkly with the machinery of my own mortality. In the dwindling queue I could see and count the units, the days, being struck off before me, the cogs turning inexorably, the second hand approaching midnight. It was the same divine retribution I had been taught in church and Sunday school but failed to connect with. Your day will come. It *will* happen to you.

Reality was suddenly, shockingly real.

And then in a matter of seconds, with two vicious, scalding whips, it was over. And I went back to my lessons. To my afterlife. Opened my books, wrote down the words from the blackboard, and paid attention. Pretended to.

I wondered how it might have looked to a passer-by outside the rainy window. The winding punishment line. The windmilling arm coming down again and again and again.

Saved

Mr Crichton took us for registration and RE. He was a wood-work teacher and an active member of the church in civilian life. A perfectly agreeable fellow: not too intimidating or too approachable. Neither dreary, nor eccentric. Or charismatic, for that matter. Middle-aged. He had a gap-toothed smile. I quite liked him. He was a teacher. End of.

Our class, 1D, numbered about thirty and comprised exclusively native Gaelic speakers. This meant that we all came from the rural villages. If you lived outwith a fifteen-mile radius of Stornoway – Ness, West Side, Uig, South Lochs – you had to board during the week in a hostel in the town. These ultra-rurals, a kind of juvenile Foreign Legion, were referred to as Hostiles.

Having a captive audience, it's likely that Mr Crichton saw his morning half-hour with us as an opportunity to flex his evangelism before adjourning to the familiarity and sanctuary of the wood-work room, with its benches, mallets, chisels and gouges. Perhaps he thought of it as a kind of spiritual husbandry. Plant the seed, nurture young souls and ultimately prepare us for the hereafter.

One day, he distributed long strips of white card to each pupil. Daily we were to write down and memorise successive verses from a chapter in Corinthians in the Gaelic bible. After a day or two, confident that we were on-message, he let us get on with it under our own initiative. So it went on – and on, it seemed, to no end.

Until, a couple of weeks later, he began a lesson by briskly and cheerfully asking a random pupil to recite the chapter by heart. Given that we had been instructed to learn it, it's hard to explain why this was so unexpected. The startled boy stuttered, clammed up and looked at his desk. The air tightened. The next boy said

33

nothing. Next, nothing. Next. Blank. Me. Nothing. Next... And as he made his way through the class, his initial enthusiasm, tinged with irritation and disappointment, began to lose momentum, to slow, stall and droop into resignation. The tension slackened.

In contrast, each pupil became emboldened by a sense of safety in numbers. Progressively more confident and assured. Defiant in their failure. There was a different dynamic. A sense that the power had shifted from teacher to pupil.

After a certain apex, it felt that even if you *had* memorised the text, it might have been difficult or uncomfortable to acknowledge. Because now there was class solidarity. It would have broken ranks. Breached the united front. You were one of us, not one of him.

From which point, he knew the game was up. So he gave up. Voice heavily accented with defeat, he asked if anybody had done the work. There was an unembarrassed silence.

And then Joan Marion stood up. And recited the entire chapter in Gaelic from start to finish, without pause or stumble. And there was another prolonged silence. A different silence.

It seemed, looking at Mr Crichton, that he was deeply moved. As if he had been vindicated, validated, rescued. That, at least, one soul had been saved. That it *had* been worth it. There was a lump in his throat. He nodded his head, as if in agreement, did not speak, swallowed and marched out of the classroom.

We looked at each other. Where did he go?

Several minutes later he came back, walked up to Joan Marion's desk and gave her a pile of money. Doubtless she would have further reward in Heaven. But I also got to thinking that on that day she saved us all.

Skye Walk

Has anyone ever actually *seen* Skye? I have. But it's a fair question. *Eilean a' Cheò* (The Misty Isle), cloaked in perennial dampness, curtained with rain, is seldom that visible. All these postcard views are taken through a narrow weather window.

Aside from the brief moon-landing in Kyle and Mallaig, I had never been off the Isle of Lewis, so one summer my cousin Uisdean, *his* cousin Donnie Mhurchaidh and I decided to go on a camping holiday to Skye. We ordered a second-hand tent and rucksacks from the *Exchange & Mart*. Mine was ex-army, khaki, canvas, with a flat metal crosspiece against the back. Also, collapsible aluminium pans, plastic mugs, gas stove and the like. It was a serious business and we were going to do this properly.

We would take the *Loch Seaforth* to Kyle of Lochalsh and walk the length of the island first to the main town of Portree and then Uig, where we would get the ferry to Harris and the bus to Stornoway. A hiking holiday. Yes, that's what it would be.

The weather was freakishly clear, sunny and warm when we arrived at Kyle in the late afternoon and took the ferry for the short trip over-the-sea-to-Skye. To Kyleakin. There's debate as to whether Skye is an island anymore now that there is a bridge across. It's a bit of a cake-and-eat-it thing. Having the far-flung, remote, tourist-friendly, romantic connotations of island-ness with all the accessibility of the mainland. If it were conjoined by a narrow isthmus it would be a peninsula, but because it is connected artificially by human agency, it remains an island. They say.

What we hadn't reckoned with was the volume of tourist traffic on Skye. We thought it would be like Lewis. It wasn't. The main road was a properly maintained two-way system. Not single track with passing places. Lewis, at that time, was an underfunded off-shore colony of Ross and Cromarty District Council, while Skye was Inverness-shire.

This first day was the overture that established both the key and time signature for our journey. Things began to announce themselves. Themes that would develop in the comprehensive scope of the days ahead. These included the hard and unforgiving smack and clump of boots on tarmac, the increasing weight of our rucksacks, the narrow strapping on mine and particularly the metal cross-frame. The weather was hot and still.

From the moment we began following the road, it was akin to walking on the hard shoulder of a motorway. An industrial conveyor belt of traffic whipped past in an unbroken stream. As we plodded on like mules in single file, cars, vans, buses and lorries whumped by in an aural strobe. Our progress seemed barely discernible. We could look back and confirm that we had moved on, advanced. But the experience was that of a treadmill. Who knew a mile could be so long? And that there could be so many of them? A cyclist floated past, with a faint whirr as if he were airborne. So light.

It became dawningly apparent, without ever reaching conscious articulation, that this would not be recreation or leisure. This would be endurance.

It was our shortest day on the hoof. Soon, we would need to camp for the night. But nowhere seemed suitable until, finally, in some tussocky, nondescript no man's land somewhere near Broadford, we ran out of options and choosiness and made a decision. Here. Beside a huge pile of spoil and aggregate from a road-widening scheme. There was no running water nearby but there was a ditch.

Now, stationary, in the sultry evening air, we were at the mercy of the midges. Not the worst I had experienced, but bad enough to make putting the tent up an ordeal. If this truncated first day could also be described as an aperitif for the days ahead, it was an appetiser for which we would, literally, become the main course.

For the first time in my life I was away from home without my family. And I felt physically sick. Homesick. I had never tasted this flavour of melancholy before. The tears bubbled and bulged behind my closed eyelids and leaked into my sleeping bag as I contemplated the coming days.

We might only have been a couple of hours on the road but were exhausted and fell asleep to the automated drone of traffic nyeeeaaawing past. I had imagined the nocturnal drumming of snipe in flight as the soundtrack to our slumber. It seemed I would have to adapt.

Sleep, however fitful, is restorative. We'd had the reality check and faced the new day with a sense of purpose and resolve. It was now a challenge. The road ahead beckoned. New things to see, to explore and discover. How far could we walk in a day? How soon would we get to Portree?

But rebranding the experience had limited success. The straps bit deeper, the frame chafed more abrasively, the road surface became harder. It was a long haul but, sandwiched between the shock of the first day and what was to come, it is largely unmemorable. The lower slopes and foothills of misery cast in the shadow of the looming peaks.

We camped on the slope of a hill. Peaceful, away from the road, beside a stream. We'd met an animated old *Sgitheanach* who, accustomed to sundry foreigners and *Sasannaich*, was thrilled that he could have a conversation in Gaelic. There being so few of us left. He knew people from Lewis from the war and the merchant navy. There were decades between us but also a closeness, a comfortable easy familiarity. Our village was full of people like him.

They say comedy is tragedy plus time. A key ingredient in this story is that none of us had a watch. In a spatial and linear sense, simply by following the road, we had direction. We had a destination and yet, because we had no sense of how much time had passed or what time of day it was, we were disorientated. Lost in time, so to speak.

Another missing component, which would have enabled us to assimilate and manage the challenge, was distance. Aside from the very occasional road sign, we had no idea how far we had travelled or how far there was to go. The only metric was how much we were suffering. Not a reliable indicator. With the late start, I estimate that the first day could only have been about three miles. The second, maybe ten. By that simple calculus, at the start of the third day, Portree was at least twenty miles away. But, of course, we didn't know any of that.

In retrospect, we guessed that – by accident – we must have got up at about five or six o'clock the following morning. And because we were awake, we had to get up and get going. The clue that it was so early was in the eerie lightness of the traffic. All the houses still had their curtains drawn.

To the tyranny of the blank page add the indifference of the open road.

Misery is incremental. As it ratcheted up, simultaneously we acclimatised. Just not enough. There were no sudden twinges, aches, pulled muscles, injuries. In the same way that, by looking back, we got a sense of the distance travelled, I could reflect on how I felt coming off the ferry in Kyle, and how I felt now. Like I was in the wrong body. Or in the most ill-fitting clothes imaginable. Tight, bone-bendingly constrictive, woven from skin-scraping wire wool, chafing in all the wrong places. Iron shoes. The metal X against my back a vertical, portable rack. A petty crucifixion.

In *The Ipcress File*, under a brutal, sensory interrogation, Michael Caine as Harry Palmer clamps and works a bent nail inside his fist so that the pain will distract him, stop him losing consciousness and becoming programmed, brainwashed. The straps and the metal frame – the cross I had to bear – biting into my shoulders and blistering my spine and shoulder blades, were now beginning to serve a similar function, ensuring that I was never going to lapse into enjoyment.

Further, now my feet fought the pain in my back and shoulders with more pain. Redistributed pain. Socialist pain. A pain panorama. Blisters began to blossom on my heels. Several times we stopped that day, once under a bridge, to soak our feet, change socks, put on extra pairs and pretend we didn't have to walk anymore. Before carrying on. How much more, how far before I breach the pain barrier?

The grim purgatory obliterated all other memories of that awful journey. What we said, where we stopped to eat, the epic, gorgeous landscape, everything. In the classic TV series *The Wire*, the prison inmates cope under the creed that irrespective of the length of the sentence, you only ever serve two days: the day you go in and the day you get out. It can be applied to the two poles of this day. The cool, dewy, morning departure and the stifling, early-evening arrival in Portree with the heat radiating off the road, rising from the earth. In between was the vacuum, the merciless experience, which we had to discount.

We tottered round the outskirts and soon, miraculously, found a perfect, flat green space beside a stream, where we put up the tent. I was already trying to get into my sleeping bag when a pleasant young man sauntered towards us and told us, gently, a little apologetically, that we couldn't camp here. That this was a golf course.

So we broke camp and, following his advice and directions, limped in towards town to a place among some trees. On our way, an elderly couple in cardigans watched us approach and just after we passed, I heard the woman say, "Poor wee soul."

Creakingly, we descended into a shaded, dappled glade with a little stream. Our walk was over, we had reached our destination. Sanctuary.

But we weren't going to get off that easily. The midges came out in such density that the air itself fought for space among them. It took on a granular texture. The bites proliferated. In my hair, under my collar, inside my nostrils and Y-fronts. There were bites on my bites. I could have wept with frustration but I was too tired even for that.

In all these miles we never once stuck out our thumbs to solicit a lift. Why? We were too shy.

Next day, we took a bus tour round the north of the island on what was probably the hottest day in the history of Skye since it was formed millennia ago in a volcanic maelstrom. We were, I would guess, the youngest people on the bus by a minimum of forty years. There was no air conditioning and all the windows were closed. In this airless, mobile greenhouse we poached pinkly in our own sweat. Prickled with midge bites.

Thankfully, we stopped for a break at a viewpoint in Staffin and everyone got out for a while. When we got back on board, the driver decided to open the windows along the roof of the bus. Oh, the blessed, blessed relief. Especially when we got moving again. Things were looking up.

And then, as we settled in ready to leave, one of the old dears asked the driver to shut them all again. Which he did.

Scorched

On leaving school, my first job was working on the quay for the Stornoway Pier and Harbour Commission. Aided by some low-level nepotism (my father), Uisdean and I were hired for the summer before college to paint the ramp for the new ferry.

This was the apparatus that heralded the new age of RoRo (roll-on, roll-off) ferries. Hitherto, vehicles had to be either winched into the ship's hold by crane or lowered down from the deck on a hydraulic platform. It was painfully slow. But now the ramp could be raised and lowered to meet the ship's upturned open bow and the cars simply drove off. It was revolutionary. A kind of marriage between ferry and bridge.

Some of old Stornoway was still left quayside. John the Barber's, for example, and the paint store, which became our headquarters.

Along with haircuts, The Barber was also a one-time chairman of the Commission. Whatever his attributes, he could be irascible, insensitive and unpleasant. One day, he came into the office and by the time he left, the secretary was bubbling in tears. My dad went to comfort her, put his arm around her and said, "Never you mind. I know that right at this moment you don't like John the Barber very much. But just you wait. In a very short while, you'll grow to hate him."

In recent years, one of the main growth industries in the Islands has been nostalgia. Local history societies have proliferated, there's a hugely popular publication called *Back in the Day*, and on websites like *Stornoway Now and Then*, dewy eyes pore over photos of the old town and avidly devour personal testimonies of past life. The good life.

It's quite at odds with how much of old Stornoway was,

without sentiment or ceremony, bulldozed. The old octagonal brick and corrugated iron fish-mart, one of the most distinctive buildings in the north of Scotland, vanished overnight and not a brick was preserved. Much later, the old art deco ferry terminal was diagnosed with concrete cancer and demolished. It was unsafe. For such a supposedly fragile edifice though, it resisted the diggers stubbornly for days until finally succumbing and disappearing.

Our first port of call every morning was the old watch room on the corner. It was where my father had had his first office. All battered leather chairs, occupied by battered, leathery old men. Fiddley, Iomhar, Angie Beò, Spolly, Calum Ruadh among them; there was another we called The Monkey on account of simian similarities. All of them had been in the Royal Navy during the war, and in the merchant navy after the war. All smoked roll-ups, almost all spoke Gaelic as a first language, all were approaching pensionable age and – other than going round the quay between tea breaks – their roles were not immediately apparent. I think it was as much a social service as anything. There were proper jobs to do, like replacing the greenheart fenders round the quay, which the carpenters did, and providing water for visiting ships, but other than that nothing onerous.

It was parochially, nautically Runyonesque.

Fiddley barely had a hair on his head and possessed a dry, droll demeanour like the late Chick Murray. He looked in the mirror one time and asked Uisdean, with the utmost seriousness, if he had a comb he could borrow. Uisdean couldn't risk offending this grave senior citizen, and when he offered his comb Fiddley looked in the mirror again and said that, actually, thinking about it, he might get away with it.

He would relate how he would wake most nights at four in the morning coughing his guts out and would need a cigarette to get back to sleep. Iomhar had glasses like fish-eye lenses. Billy Goat liked a drink and did plenty of it but had never been known to buy one.

There were still dockers, too. And a regular quayside clientele of people who drifted down there as if borne on the tide. To meet people they knew, see what the boats had brought in, to scavenge "a fry". Daily, we would see a small, skinny old fellow called Sgealban, still in his de-mob suit. He's captured in my mind walking towards us in the early morning, carrying an enormous fish wrapped in a newspaper under his arm.

Norwegian, Danish and Spanish trawlers were frequent visitors. The Spanish always gave my father bottles of Soberano brandy. The Scandinavians were defined by deep-sea saturation boozing whenever they hit town. It was supposed that, as much as a recreational reaction to dry weeks at sea, it was boosted and compounded by the scarcity and expense of alcoholic product back home. A kind of compensation. Here, it was cheap and available, so obliteration was the order of the day. One time they bought up Stornoway's entire supply of vodka. To be fair, they also bought huge quantities of Quality Street sweets.

We were given a raft for painting at sea level and were frequently swamped by the wash of the fishing boats that swept in and out of the harbour: *The Ripple, Kathleen, Fiery Cross, Ocean Reward, Ivy Rose, Silver Cord, Providence, Wave Crest...*

When it rained, we went round the quay picking up rubbish in the barrow, trying to look busy. Which was hard work in and of itself. Tested your creativity. We also cleaned the gents' toilets on South Beach – known as the Opera House on account of its popularity as a venue for carousing drunks. This involved hosing down the interior, taking the different denominations of often foreign coins from the cubicles and emptying a crystal avalanche of bottles from the bin.

The first day, though, we were aloft on the steel superstructure. Start at the top. We got into our boiler suits in the paint store and took the paint and brushes on site in a wheelbarrow.

The ramp was a big area of industrial steel and it would take us all summer to cover it with the thick, black, tarry, bitumen-based paint that was stockpiled in the store. Still, nobody was cracking the whip. It was a breezy, pleasant enough day with intermittent cloud cover, and that evening I had a hot face. A reaction to being in the open air, sun reflecting off the water, my fair, freckled skin. Lentiginous. To be expected. I'd get used to it.

But I didn't. Green-eyed, darker skinned Uisdean seemed to be coping just fine. He only had sight in one eye on account of sticking a *cutag* – a knife for gutting herring – right through his pupil as a toddler. That's another story. For me, it seemed to be worse on sunny days; and despite sun lotion it wasn't just hot, it was burning hot. Painful. I began to have a psychological as well as a physical reaction to the paint. I became conscious of the fumes that came off it. Could envisage them, taste them. Finally, I said that was it. I was going to hand in my notice. The next day, it wasn't quite so bad. So I stuck by it. This happened a few times.

In between were interludes like Thompson's party. Almost everyone I knew went through an incident where they had drunk themselves unconscious. Not deliberately, of course – it was just a recreational hazard. It was also something of a badge of honour. Like losing your virginity.

Thompson was Donnie's boss at the Department of Weights and Measures and, as he was about to leave, he was throwing a party. If you could call it that. Not a big deal, just a few close friends sitting on a sofa in his house drinking. We went to the pub beforehand and had a few pints. Then we got our carry-out of McEwan's Export and a bottle of Johnny Walker Red Label. On the way up to the house, we turned a corner and ran straight into Mr

Crichton, my former RE teacher, on his way back from a regular Thursday night church communion meeting. I was already drunk but, having left school, we were no longer under his jurisdiction.

Disapproval radiated off him and when he asked caustically what was in the bag, cheekily I said, "Chips." Scotch courage.

From that point on, the evening begins to descend into murk. From arriving at the suburban door, I began to sink ever deeper through an amber sea until there was only darkness illuminated by occasional luminous flashes of ocean bottom grotesques. I was *compos mentis* enough on arrival to register the domestic arrangement, sofa set-up and stylistic cues that I would recognise many years later when I watched *Abigail's Party*. I'm confident there were tank-tops and platform shoes.

Whisky, it is said, can be a civilised drink. In moderation. But there are people I know who turn into Hyde incarnate when it courses through their veins. With too much, I fear I may be one of them.

What fragments of memory can I salvage from the shipwreck of that evening? Only, generically, sitting on a sofa. And going into the bathroom, falling into the bath while having a pee and being hauled out. Most vividly, a raucous sing-along chorus, accompanied by thumping knees, like an insane tape loop that went round and round in my head as if echoing in an empty bucket.

Durum-a-doo-a-durum-a-day
Durum-a-doo-a-daddio
Durum-a-doo-a-durum-a-day
The day we went to Rothesay-o

That's it. For the rest, I would have to rely on witnesses.

My mother was standing at the end of my bed. She was holding the pale cream top with a crossed drawstring that I had been wearing. Now it had expressionist orangey-red stripes caked down the front. She was saying, "What the hell is this?" I didn't know. It was seven o'clock in the morning and time to get up and go to work. I could imagine feeling significantly better crawling from the rubble of a bombed building.

A meat cleaver had split my skull but I had somehow survived. Catatonic, I avoided eye contact and speech, skipped breakfast, and about fifteen minutes later my lift stopped at the end of the path in front of our house. Uisdean was driving, practising for his test. His dad, who worked as a warper in Kenneth Mackenzie's Harris Tweed mill, was the co-driver in the front seat and my Uncle Seonaidh, who was a fireman at the aerodrome, was in the back. It was the longest seven miles in history. Normally, I would have stayed in the car until Seonaidh was dropped off at the 'drome, but I asked to be let out in town. As the car pulled off, I ran across the road and projectile vomited over the low sea wall.

As dazed as if I had been whacked in the back of the head with a shovel, I wandered through the deserted car park along South Beach to the watch room. On the way, I came across a pile of pornographic magazines by the sea wall. Probably from a trawler. Ordinarily, at that age, in these puritan times, this would have represented an unimaginable treasure trove. To be stashed under your mattress and cherished as a rich rhythmic resource. So it is a testimony to the severity of my condition that I browsed the acres of bare flesh, the creamy breasts, the dreamy half-closed beckoning eyes, the lurid centrefolds, with complete disinterest.

When Uisdean arrived at work, he told me that himself and Donnie had carried me from the taxi, knocked and left me at the door. By some improbable coincidence, my parents were out. Only my brother Iain was in. Later, he described trying to put me to bed. He asked why I was only wearing one shoe.

I belonged in a hospital, not at work. Not up a steel ladder with a gallon of bitumen paint. I asked Uisdean to cover for me and locked myself in the inner cupboard in the paint store, where I curled up, foetus-like, on the cold cement floor and went to sleep. Around midday, I woke up and threw up. My body was saturated with toxins and had to expectorate it, sweat it, expel it by all means available. Then I got the idea of flushing out my system. Throughout the afternoon I drank water, threw up, drank water, threw up, drank water… until, by the end of the working day, I was only half dead.

That was Thompson's party.

So the work and the summer wore on, and now my skin became a battleground. I tried Vaseline, barrier cream, but I still burned. A windy, wet or overcast day was best and there were enough of these for me to bear it. Cling on. Getting paid was a decent incentive, too.

But there came a reckoning. A hot, airless Friday where the paint fumes boiled in invisible, toxic clouds out of the can and off my brush. Strange that the smell was perfectly tolerable – a masculine, creosote-y tang – but my skin felt like it was being acid-etched. I began to think of it as a not-so-distant cousin of mustard gas.

There was a big wedding that night and we were all going. Incredibly, a girl around our age, called Sìne a' Lasgainn, was getting married. But as clocking off time drew near, my epidermis was in such extremis that there was only one place I could go. Accident and Emergency. I don't think I could have been in any more pain if someone had gone over my face with a blowtorch. In the open air, in the shade, with a light breeze, it was on the outer fingertips edge of bearable. In an enclosed space, a room, a car, it became a lava field.

I sat back in a chair as the nurse basted my face with the most effective and advanced medical liniment they had: olive oil. Only available in pharmacies at that time. I suppose there is a culinary connection. I've heard people described as having a roast beef complexion or a face like a side of ham. I was more like crispy bacon.

The condiment did ease the pain a fair bit, but I could only bear to look once in the mirror at the yacht-varnished, mottled, walnut-and-conker gargoyle that I had become. Obviously, the wedding dance was off. In any case, I didn't want to alarm anyone or ruin the bride's big day.

Over the weekend, my face hardened into a crust. I could tap it with my fingernail like a veneer. And as I had nothing to smile or laugh about, I was able to avoid any painful crack or crinkle that might occur as a result. I was the man in the ginger mask. Over the coming days, my skin began to shed lizard-like, in crisp flakes. As newly pink as a shelled prawn underneath.

That year, I had won the school prize for art. But, around the same time, I declined to attend the prize-giving ceremony for that, too.

Rat Patrol

In March 1973, the school prepared for an expedition to the Shiant Islands off the coast of Harris, then owned by Nigel Nicolson. We wrote to him at Sissinghurst in Kent to respectfully ask permission – or at least give fair warning of our intent – and received a gracious reply giving us his blessing. Since that time, under the benevolent, enlightened stewardship of his son, Adam, the Shiants have become ever more prominent on the ecological and literary map.

The trip was organised by the biology department, and the primary reason for our visit was to be there when the puffins arrived on their spring migration. We were to observe and appreciate the great seabird spectacle, count numbers and develop our ornithological field practice. I'd only ever seen the plucky sea parrot in pictures or washed up on the shoreline.

A secondary motive was rat research. The islands were notoriously infested. Legend had it that even cats, once introduced as a natural predator, were eventually overrun. The biology textbooks of the day noted that both species, black (*Rattus rattus*) and brown (*Rattus norvegicus*), were present in abundance. Two tribes. One fanciful theory as to how they originally got there was from a stray shipwrecked galleon from the Spanish Armada.

And so a subset of us formed a rat-catching patrol, for which I volunteered. It was something to look forward to. A mission with real purpose. I don't have the fear or repulsion that many people have for rats. I'm no Winston Smith. That said, I didn't come across them very often and those I did were mostly dead. The cats at home saw to that.

We were advised in advance on essential kit: changes of clothing, stout boots and so on. Buy a cagoule. Also, importantly, bring a musical instrument if you have one. I decide to take my clarinet. Perhaps the Shiants will be the perfect setting to play *Stranger on the Shore*. At seventeen, although surrounded, cosseted and buffeted by family, school friends and community, it is entirely possible to be lonely. In plain sight. I do believe I have an aptitude for it.

That winter refused to go quietly or quickly. The weather was thrawn. Defiant. Ill-tempered. March flew into April in a flurry of savage squalls of hail and snow. The pale sun never prolonged or intense enough to warm or dry the sodden earth. The damp, raw air scoured your skin, chilled your bones. Anvil clouds hung in the sky.

We took a bus the thirty-six miles from Stornoway to Tarbert, Harris, and there assembled on the pier to board the Scalpay fishing boat, the *Village Maid*. The Scalpachs used to graze their sheep on the Shiants, so there was regular (if infrequent) marine traffic to the islands. It's hard to imagine such an educational excursion being even legal now. Over a dozen kids, without lifejackets, being ferried the sixteen or so nautical miles across the exposed, tidal rip of the open Minch, huddled on the deck of a pitching drifter.

The Shiants comprise three uninhabited islands. Two of these, Garbh Eilean (Rough Island) and Eilean Taigh (House Island), are joined by a narrow, tongue-twisting, shingle isthmus. Eilean Mhuire (Mary's Island) is separate. Less accessible but seemingly more arable. It is ridged with *feannagan* (raised lazy beds) for cultivating crops. But no one ever lived there.

The group is a geological, Celtic cousin of Fingal's Cave on Staffa and the Giant's Causeway in Northern Ireland. This is most apparent on Garbh Eilean, which is defined by its vertiginous cliffs, a skyward thrust of basalt pillars a couple of hundred feet high. Its foothills, a scree of outsize boulders collapsed from some primeval disaster, provide a stony warren for puffins to burrow and breed.

Overhead, among the guillemots, kittiwakes and fulmars, great skuas wheel and plunge. The avian antonym of the neighbourly puffin. A menacing and pugnacious winged villain.

At sea level, relentless, unstoppable, the Minch bores through the island's natural arch, the waves fanning out in a graceful arc with each slow, wheezing surge.

The shingle strip between the islands is the only landing point, and we are shuttled ashore in groups on an inflatable dinghy. We set up camp on Eilean Taigh behind the titular house, pitch tents, dig drainage ditches and dry our clothes on guy ropes and across ridge poles. If you aren't doing anything, it is cold. If you stop because you are tired, you *get* cold. If you get wet, you get colder. Best avoided. As if you have a choice. Only the hormonal fever of adolescence keeps me warm over these days. But it's the wrong kind of warm.

And we settle in. Get paired off in tents, sort our sleeping bags, collect basic supplies. Learn how to use a Primus stove. From across the camp, during a brief weather respite – a flare of sunlight between strafing hailstorms – I hear *Drive-in Saturday* by David Bowie coming over a radio. Forever fixed in my memory to evoke this time and this place. Like a message from the future: alien, unearthly in the context of this weather-stricken offshore outpost.

The following day, after breakfast and a briefing, we set off to lay our traps. These are rectangular steel-wire cages with a spring-loaded door at one end, held open by a latch on the cage floor. A piece of rotten mackerel is thrown in for bait and when the rat enters, its weight trips the latch and the door springs shut behind it. It's equivalent to an onshore lobster pot.

To begin with, we find random spots close at hand, only in later days to climb the steep hairpins up Garbh Eilean as we extend our range.

The team leader is Dr Peter Hopkins, our biology teacher. The others are the two Margarets, and my classmate Donald Cook, who is given the task of taking the rats out of the cage and holding them for execution. For this, he wears elbow-length asbestos gloves. Dr Hopkins assures us that the most humane, instantaneous method of despatch is to cut the spinal cord from the back of the neck with surgical scissors. Which, mercifully, is his job.

So, methodically, we set about our business.

When we return to the traps the following morning, a rat scuttles back and forth in the first cage we laid. Scaly-tailed, slightly bedraggled, confused, bewildered; bumbling and bumping against the wire walls. It seems no more than an enormous mouse. Only when grabbed in the asbestos fist does it transform – with a metal-rending, terrified shriek – into a barely containable feral clot. Skreeeeeking, it scrabbles and struggles, violently twitching and trembling, baring curved yellow incisors.

His own teeth clamped, Donald holds it at arm's length until the doctor wields the scissors and, with a steely clip, summons an instant silence. The little animal's head almost falls off. Semi-decapitated, it is dropped into a polythene specimen bag and sealed up. One down...

You'll get used to anything, I suppose, if you do it often enough. Horrors become normalised and assimilated, pleasures diminished and trivialised. Senses numbed by the ever-thickening skin. But we remain tattooed with the first experience, the unscrapable original ever legible on the parchment. Life's rich palimpsest.

In all the times we set the traps, not once do we fail to catch a rat. Often, there are two in the same cage. We catch black ones and brown ones, across a sombre spectrum from sooty to dusky to tawny. From relatively small to gross and heavy-bellied. Well fed. Over the days, Donald finds it easier and quicker to just whack the back of their heads on a nearby rock. There is an endless, inexhaustible supply of them.

One of the Margarets becomes ill with suspected appendicitis and the lifeboat is sent from Stornoway for her. The crew leaves us an unlabelled bottle of Navy-issue dark rum and despite us being underage, the teachers offer everyone a virgin tot. It is the ultimate, perhaps the only way to appreciate Navy rum. Sat around a campfire of roaring driftwood with the cold, salt sea and the black, windy night at your back. The right kind of warm.

Frustratingly, the puffins are late and the main purpose of our expedition is unfulfilled. We don't get to see the sky-blackening, whirling clouds of them, the rainbowed beaks. Not a single one. And, after a few days, wind-burned and weary, we leave the Shiants with our cargo of dead rodents.

Back in the lab, in their poly bags I notice all the fleas and parasites have now left the sunken rats. When the fleas die, will still smaller parasites leave them? And on, and on?

And we discover something interesting, too. On examination, we find that the brown rats aren't brown; they're black. They are all black rats, merely with tonal variations. Blondes and brunettes. The island belongs exclusively to *Rattus rattus*. It is a minor scientific breakthrough.

And some kind of parable. A subliminal message about appearance and assumption.

Post-script: Following a four-year eradication project by the RSPB, in March 2018 – forty-five years to the month after our expedition – the Shiant Islands were officially declared rat-free.

Mùirneag

The highest point on North Lewis is Mùirneag. At a mere 814 feet, it isn't even a mountain. Yet its flattened, rounded "M" profile is visible from an improbable distance because it rises out of the flat, featureless, loch-riddled moorland that stretches from the Butt of Lewis to the Barvas Hills. To the west, the Atlantic vanishes off to a horizon line; to the east, the Minch stretches till it breaks on the shores of the North West Highlands.

From the top you can see the extent of the island and grasp the emptiness. The straggle of villages that nibble the coast but shun the vacant hinterland of the interior.

Until the post-war years, the open moor was a resource. In the seasonal sweep and cycle of subsistence living, cattle would be taken there for summer pasture and families would decant to the numerous *àirighean* (sheilings or bothies) on the shores of isolated lochs. A literature of story and song arose from the paradox of community and isolation of this experience.

When poring over Ordnance Survey maps for our next fishing expedition, we always noted the miniature communities harboured by remote lochs strewn across this nowhere. But we knew that, on the ground, there was barely a vestige of human habitation left. Only collapsed heaps of stone overgrown by a skin of peat, rushes, heather, lichen, bog cotton and moss. *Mòine, luachair, fraoch, crotal, canach is còinneach.* A silent Gaelic mantra from the botanical codex.

The maps were an X-ray that revealed the past. The bones. An anatomical diagram of lost livelihoods and vanished summers.

Mùirneag didn't look that far away out of our scullery window. It was just behind Iain Dhollaidh's house, whose chimney pots poked over the immediate horizon like a collie's ears. Years earlier, as small children, provisioned with some sweets and a bottle of lemonade, we had set off one morning to climb it. After surmounting fences, crossing streams and heroically arriving at the house, we were dismayed to find that Mùirneag was no nearer than when we had left home. It had stayed where it was in the distance, a backstop to a tonal exercise of receding horizon lines. Not least, it was now verifiably on the other side of the Gress river.

My younger brother Iain and first cousin Coinneach had identified a loch at the foot of Mùirneag on the Tolsta side and decided that it qualified as excellent. There was no evidence for this beyond the faintest echo of hearsay. But we were resolutely faithful to a creed that the further away the loch, the better the fishing. Probably from some kind of subconscious Presbyterian logic, based on ratios of suffering-to-reward. No pain, no gain. Or, more rationally, that less fished meant more fish.

We were in our mid-teens. And, by that age, had evaluated the distance. We now knew we could take the peat road that followed the Gress river as it rose and continue after the road ran out until we reached the dam, where we could jump the weir and get across. Thereafter, the traverse of the open moor. We would go over Mùirneag, down the east side and camp by the loch.

It is the summer holidays and we leave early on a still, overcast afternoon. Walk the road and the beaten track, up the river, over the gruelling, energy-sucking ground; climb and descend, and reach the loch by evening. In the damp, oppressive air, sticky with sweat, we put up the two-person, single-skinned cotton tent on a flattish, spongey piece of ground by the water's edge. The faded orange a colour-wheel complement to the muted greens of moss and grass.

The clouds become too heavy for the sky and begin to condense, deliquesce and drip as if from a gentle squeeze on a soaked sponge. The midges track our blood-warmed breath, trail our body heat and surround us like smoke. We set out a couple of rods with bubble floats and try to outrun them by taking an otter board round the loch.

An otter board is a rectangular plank of wood, a couple of feet wide, lead-weighted along the long edge so that it sits upright in the water. In profile, it's wedge-shaped at both ends and, when pulled barge-like along the bank by a long cord, the bladed board will angle away from the shore and trail a fly-cast. No skill required. It's a basic but effective means of covering a lot of loch.

But not that effective, because we don't catch anything. On the board or on the rods. The conditions are against us. The perennial, timeless excuse in the fisherman's repertoire. You need a good ripple on the water.

Now the precipitation becomes a faint drizzle. *Smùid, uisge-mìn, braon, ceòthran, drùis...* the Gaelic lexicon for rain begins to riffle. *Sil, dìle, tuil, bùirseach...* The stagnant air stirs and a rising breeze whisks the midges away. With our enthusiasm as yet undampened, we meditate on a plan for the next day until the light fades to dusk and we crawl into the tent and our sleeping bags. And quickly fall asleep.

And as quickly – it seems – wake up. The lower half of my bag is soaking wet. The tent is dripping, rain dropping along the ridge pole, pooling on the groundsheet, the cotton fabric translucent in patches, mottling the early daylight. Iain and Coinneach have woken, too. There is nothing for it. We have to get up.

Stuffed into rucksacks overnight our clothes are, at least, partially dry. So, constricted between the tapered, narrow wet walls, in the half light, we contort into layers: check shirts, hand-knitted bobbin socks and jumpers, jeans, those cotton cagoules with the large front pocket and, of course, wellies. It's decent outdoor kit but not the climate-proof, language-bending technical clobber that now passes as minimum standard: the Gore-Texed, lightweight but hard-wearing, waterproof but breathable, warm but cool ...

The rain drops into our mugs of tea and the day stretches ahead over a vague horizon. We orbit the loch with the otter board once more. In the rain. And make another plan. In the rain. We decide to take the board, leave the tent, the gear and the rods, climb Mùirneag again and head for Loch Ghriais at the source of the Gress river. In the rain.

So we haul ourselves up the hill and take a bearing from the Ordnance Survey cairn at the top to a distant hollow of water in a dark blur of moor. And head into a water-logged south-westerly on a diagonal descent along the back of Mùirneag.

Baptised in bleakness, the sodden, saturated, shelterless Lewis moorland is a psychological as much as a physical landscape. We have endured such days before, huddled under the banks of a loch, watching a bubble-float. On the verge of hallucination as the amber water laps and wears away the stones. The rain infiltrating each fold and crevice of clothing and skin. Nowhere dry enough to sit on. Breathing rain. Morale diluting by osmosis.

If we cannot ignore it, we must accept it, even as it commands our attention and the cold attempts to clutch us in its clammy hand. It trickles down the backs of our necks, our trousers wallpapered to our thighs. Only walking, movement, keeps the damp chill at bay. Sweat and rain intermingles on the floodplain of our bodies.

The terrain is defiant, unforgiving, broken moorland. It isn't a linear transit over land, it is three-dimensional. Through, over and around. Lochans, sunken bogs, peat escarpments (hags), knee-high heather. Like some ponderous, slow suicide. One foot in front of the other. Getting nearer. One further step away. From some kind of weather sanctuary. Keep going, though. To the end. What end?

Absorbed within ourselves, imprisoned in our chosen mission, we ignore wider issues. No one thinks to ask: what the fuck are we doing? We have had to get up because the tent is flooded. We can't sleep there. We have no refuge to return to. We are exposed on a barren, desolate expanse of bog, miles from anywhere. And instead of packing up and going home, we are heading deeper into the moor because there might be a better chance of fish on another loch.

God knows when we reach Loch Ghriais. Grimly, we set off round the swollen, rain-bloated expanse with the otter board. We do not have a watch. Time can only be measured by hunch. The sun is lost. Not a trace of it. Daylight is almost continuous in summer, so it could be late morning or mid-afternoon.

I catch a small trout and throw it back into the rain-swept loch.

And then, about two-thirds of the way round, an unusual rounded geographical feature like a small hillock comes into view on the bank. As we approach, it assumes basic architectural proportions and becomes an *àirigh*. A windowless, drystone bee-hive construction with a domed, densely sprouted turf roof and a wooden door. Which isn't locked. Inside are two recessed bunk-beds with heather mattresses and the crumbling, desiccated, rusted remnants of old provisions. Impossible to say when it had been last occupied. Probably years.

Most importantly, unbelievably, it is dry.

For a moment, relief and despair collide. We know we have been saved and can simultaneously acknowledge openly the desperate situation we've been in. We can stay here. It is the only thing we can do. But we realise, too, that now we have to go back over the moor, over Mùirneag, collect the tent, sleeping bags, food and gear and come all the way back to this *àirigh*. In the rain.

Energy, commitment and concentration are harnessed when you have no choice. The body as a vehicle mechanically functions without the inconvenience and intrusion of thought, of decision. It's a pure state. We are resolved and resilient.

Painstakingly, we head back through the hours, climb Mùirneag, descend the other side and at last approach the loch and the tent. At which point I experience a shaking, unstoppable, violent hunger. It borders on rage. I feel as if I have been hollowed out; that I am about to implode around an interior vacuum. I tear frantically, desperately, at the rucksack in the tent and fumble for the extra-large tin of spam I know is there. With trembling fingers, I turn the attached key, spiral the tin ribbon to take the top off, pull out the entire gelatinous, greasy pink oblong with my bare hands, sink my teeth into it and gulp half of it down in large gobbets. I pass it round and it is gone.

Then we pack up the gear and the tent like so much wet laundry and, for the fourth time in twenty-four hours, with the additional burden of rucksacks, climb Mùirneag and head once more, step by laborious step, into the rain and wind. At least this time there is a point. We have a destination. A motive. An end.

It must be well into the evening when we stagger along the bank of Loch Ghriais to the *àirigh*. Using the gas stove, we make a fire from some dry heather and peats that are inside and, to a degree, dry out in the dim smokehouse we have created. The sense of achievement is towering. The self-congratulation colossal. The self-delusion epic. Our good fortune, masquerading as survival skills, aptitude, fortitude and endurance, obliterates the idiocy of the escapade.

Sleep closes in like instant nightfall. Oblivion.

The following morning the rain has stopped. Overnight, deep blue chasms have been excavated in the sky. There is a fresh, drying wind, occasional startling bursts of bright sunshine, clarity and airiness. Visibility has extended, distance expanded. All we have to do is follow the course of the Gress downstream until we reach the dam. Cross that and we are back on the beaten track.

Along the side of the loch, we come across the remnants of a weather balloon, downed overnight. The apparatus is all geometry, engineering, cantilevered aluminium angles. Collapsed like the broken bones of an ambitious kite or a small biplane, it drags shredded latex and a tangle of cords. A pathetic, busted, puppet Icarus. Incongruous. Alien. Ridiculous. Somehow symbolic.

In Memoriam

Coinneach Maclennan 1959 – 1977

Leathered

For me, going to Gray's School of Art in Aberdeen in 1974 was what is now called a cluster-fuck. A relentless sequence of bad decisions that propagated worse ones in an uncontrollable chain reaction. More like a fission-fuck, actually. Amid the wider fiasco of my young life, I remember it with a blend of mortification and grim detachment. Or whatever the opposite of nostalgia is.

It was silhouetted and enacted against an acute shortage of student accommodation. There was also a national sugar shortage which, while hardly a crisis, seems wryly symbolic of this dystopian past.

Our lodgings on Forrest Avenue were run by a Mrs Crook and geared to optimum revenue generation. I had to share a room – and a bed – with my cousin Uisdean. The attic conversion housed four students in one room. My friend Teddy, who was over six feet tall, couldn't stand upright in his quarters, an upstairs bunker accessed through the kitchen then a steep ladder. Others were shoved into whatever available space there was. Generously, all rooms had coin-operated meters for two-bar electric fires. Heat, like sugar, was finite, rationed and not always available.

A few months in, I cracked. Mortal drunk one night, sometime after midnight, I howled like a wounded dog outside the front door and woke the whole street. It got us thrown out and I ended up on a mattress on the floor in a shared room in a squat. There, to highlight the accommodation crisis, we were photographed looking glum in our pyjamas on the front steps, for a Scottish tabloid. It couldn't have been much more pathetic.

There were three of us in our room. Nightly, we would light a fire and burrow into our sleeping bags, the contents of our suitcases emptied on top for insulation. Only to wake in the morning, frost spidering the inside of the thin windows, ossified by the cold, with the immediate prospect of hypothermia in the desperate few minutes before you got dressed and could reclaim body temperature. I know the gulags were bad; all I'm saying is, I've been to Aberdeen.

The situational entropy was epitomised by my brief boxing career.

It was the age of kung fu, presided over by the ghost of Bruce Lee, and I had joined a karate club. Then, as a challenge, a friend who was in the University boxing club invited me to his gym. There was sparring in the ring with big padded gloves and, although you did get hit intermittently, it wasn't so bad. Maybe people pulled their punches but I did okay.

Afterwards, someone suggested that, because I was "quite quick", I could join the boxing team for their imminent trip to Dublin and the annual British University Championships. There was a vacancy: they didn't have a featherweight. It was an unprecedented stroke of luck. Ireland! I'd never been abroad.

Only one guy was reluctant to admit me: the team captain. Inexplicably, irrationally, annoyingly, he didn't want to see me "get hurt" and finally agreed only if I could get down from featherweight to bantamweight. This was under eight stones, seven pounds. You just stopped eating for a week or two and lost a couple of pounds. They'd all done it.

I can trace the stomach problems that dogged me for perhaps fifteen years back to this special time. From then, a staple part of my diet became antacids: variously Aludrox, Asilone, Polycrol, Milk of Magnesia, Gaviscon and, latterly, Tagamets. Twice, I would be X-rayed, inconclusively, for an ulcer until, somewhere along the line, when Aberdeen was a distant memory, buried like radioactive waste, it eased off and stopped.

The famishing fortnight up until the championships went by at glacial speed. From the overnight minibus to Dublin survives the embedded memory of lavish, technicolour fry-ups in the strip-light glare of Formica table food-stops. The Falls Road in Belfast on Sunday night was a war zone. Around midnight, we arrived in the Fair City itself.

Yet another breakfast-less morning saw the weigh-in, which I passed – if that's the right word – followed by a fantasy-become-reality lunch of steak and chips that gave me jack-knifing abdominal cramps. I fancy my stomach had shrivelled to the size of a walnut by then and simply couldn't process this massive, unexpected protein dump.

There was a pre-fight tactics talk: "Remember the Irish always come out really fast, guns blazing, so if you can hang on through the first couple of minutes you'll have good chances. Keep your right hand up to protect your chin… Use your jab…"

Then there are the things you can only learn for yourself. Proust said, "We don't receive wisdom; we must discover it for ourselves after a journey that no one can take for us or spare us." The wisdom I discovered was that, unlike sparring, in a real bout your hands are strapped and tightly bandaged. Then the long leather glove is rolled up as tightly as possible so that your fists effectively become weaponised. The gloves, I now saw, are to protect your hands, not to lessen damage to your opponent's cranium.

And within a few seconds of the bell, I discovered that being hit by a windmilling right cross is like being hit with a block of wood. There were to be no exploratory left jabs, after all. It was, quite literally, a stunning, staggering blow. Ringingly painful. It was just *so* fucking sore. And it was but the first of a leather blizzard.

How long did the fight last? Maybe two minutes, if that. My corner came out to meet me with a large fluffy white towel, which was soon saturated in fresh red blood.

Afterwards, my assailant came over and pleaded with me not to give up boxing. He thought I had potential. He said that he had been surprised because he caught me with a massive first punch and not only had I not gone down, it didn't even appear to bother me.

It seemed curious that this softly spoken, civil and genuinely concerned individual had only minutes before violently assaulted me.

The previous year, he had been roundly thrashed as a flyweight and when he discovered that he was scheduled to meet his nemesis in the same competition again, he panicked and ate and drank enough to bring himself up a division to bantamweight. So, fittingly, I'd been beaten to a pulp by a chicken. It was beyond failure. My humiliation was complete.

In *Raging Bull*, after being annihilated by Sugar Ray Robinson, De Niro as Jake Lamotta – who looks like he has just gone through a car windscreen and then been kicked in the head by skinheads – goes to Ray's corner and says, "You never got me down, Ray, you never got me down…" Alas, that line hadn't been written for me to deliver at that time.

Neither had Elton written *I'm Still Standing* for me to relate to and gain succour from. But let the record state that in 1974/75, I made the semi-finals of the British University Boxing Finals.

It seemed the right time to retire.

Epilogue

We went to a nightclub. I was still starving but could barely eat because my jaw ached like I'd undergone root canal without anaesthetic. Generally, my head felt as if it had been smashed apart and reassembled the wrong way. Like Lego. Mercifully, I could still drink pints. Had to.

Leathered

When we got back to Aberdeen, I went to the doctor, where I was prescribed my first dose of suspension liquid. And Librium tablets. I assumed this was gastric medication, until an older student in the squat asked if it was because my balls were dropping.

And so, as the year limped on and petered out, the prospect of abandoning life in Aberdeen and retreating home to the comfort of digging drains, painting railings or mending peat roads on bleak community work programmes in the Outer Hebrides grew ever more appealing. It was honest toil. Christ, it had to be better than this. And it just about was.

The Lost Isle

It's a long haul to Ultima Thule from Glasgow. Board the over-night train at Queen Street at eleven-thirty. Settle in. Within the hour the heating is turned off and the carriage refrigerated. The cold wakes me up. At Perth, chattering, I plead with one of the platform guards to put the heating back on. He says it can't be all that cold if I've got the window open.

Inverness, at last. Six in the morning. Still dark. Everywhere shut. Hang around hungover for the Ullapool bus at seven. Then cross-country, sixty miles to the ferry which, three and a half hours later – weather permitting – docks quayside in Stornoway, early afternoon. The only way to do it is to be young.

A fellow passenger gives me a lift home, to the village of Coll, in the Isle of Lewis, in the 1970s. He comes in for a cup of tea. Mortifyingly, there is a sheep in the front room. Welcome home.

On cue, Kennag Ruadh, the *cailleach* along the road, appears as she does every time a car parks outside our house. Astonished, apologetic, she has no idea we have a visitor. Already there is Boon-dog, whose career as a heavyweight boozer is at its peak. He's been in town since first light and is leaning forward across the back of an armchair, leather jacket, two gills of Bell's poking out from the back-pockets of his Wrangler jeans. It gives him the appearance and attitude of a gunslinger. My people.

I look back. I think back. I *am* back.

Everybody is called after their forebears – parents, aunts and uncles, grandparents, deceased relatives. The same names handed down the generations. A kind of immortality. It's not unheard of for there to be two brothers with the same name in a family: one called after the father, the other after the mother's brother, lost in the war. Inevitably Calum Mòr and Calum Beag. It's respect. It's structure. It's continuity.

And there are only a select number of names available, each with their Gaelic equivalents. You are two people. Mostly old Highland names. Donald (Dòmhnall), Murdo (Murchadh), Angus (Aonghas), Malcolm (Calum), John (Iain), Kenneth (Coinneach), Alex (Alasdair). Or *really* old ones like Evander (Iomhair). But also William (Uilleam), Norman (Tormod), Hugh (Uisdean), Roderick (Ruaraidh), George (Seòras), Allan (Ailean), Colin (Cailean)... If you are a David, you are probably from the mainland. Mark or Christopher? English. Simon? That would be an outlier, or a nickname. Paul? Nobody is called Paul. Or Joe. Saints' names. Catholic names. There aren't any.

Somehow this sectarianism *in absentia* doesn't seem to apply to girls. Mary (Màiri) is common. Along with Christine (Carstiona), Alice, Margaret (Mairead), Catherine (Catriona), Marion (Mòrag), Ann, Joan (Seonag), Janet (Seònaid), versions of Isabelle. Of course, there are no Veronicas, Jennifers, Emmas or Sophies (contd.).

If the convention of naming offspring after male forebears is inconvenienced by the birth of a girl, it can be fixed with a handy suffix. So we have Murdina, Angusina, Kenina, Calumina... even Willina. The artist Lennox Paterson has a print from the time called "Malcolmina is Home from the City".

Surnames point to your locality and your origins. Like a clan map. Macarthurs in Carloway, Macaulays in Uig, Morrisons and Murrays in Ness, Macivers in Back, Mackenzies through-out Lochs, with an enclave of Kennedys across Loch Erisort to the south. Cunninghams in Scalpay. Maclennans can be traced to the now uninhabited Isle of Scarp in Harris. Macleods and Macdonalds everywhere. Dominant.

School classrooms often have a couple of Donald Macleods,

invariably known as Donnie A and Donnie B. The well-known BBC presenter, the late Donnie B Macleod, adopts the initial professionally. I know a Donald Macdonald who lives on Macdonald Road.

My mother's maiden name was also Murray. And, no, my parents were not related. I'm named after two of her brothers who died in infancy and my father's brother, Roderick Macpherson Murray (Rory), drowned in Stornoway harbour in 1945, aged twenty-one. He was engaged to be married. Home on leave after the war. I must have survived by the law of averages.

Everybody, too, has an identifying, family patronymic in Gaelic. Like a back-story fingerprint. Coinneach Mac Alasdair Ruadh Mhurchaidh Iain an t-Saighdear – that type of thing (Kenneth, son of Red-Haired Alasdair, son of Murdo John the Soldier).

And most people have a nickname to help differentiation, usually bestowed on them in school. Typically, they have obscure or trivial origins. Some are biblical. In my year are Amos (Angus Murray), Exodus (Murdo Morrison) and Jonah (John Maciver). Caesar, too (John Campbell). *Et cetera.*

Often these handles are uncomplimentary or cruel, which makes it doubly unfortunate that they are bequeathed to the next generation. And the next. One of my mother's best friends was Peggy Rat, whose family are The Rats.

Often it is because of a single thing you did or said. One lost Sunday, a young boy is collared by the minister, who asks why he hasn't seen him in church. "No boots," he replies. And from that day hence, he would be No Boots. No matter how well-shod subsequently.

My mother's Aunt Jane (Sìne) still lived in the "black" house next door when I was a toddler. A former herring girl, she has a small porcelain boot bought in Lowestoft. I called it Gòg Miaow, which is the mispronounced Gaelic for Bròg Miaow (Cat's Boot).

And so, ever after, the aunt was called that.

If someone marries and moves to another area, their village of origin becomes their identifier. Tormod Shiabost (Shawbost), Murdo Galson, Iain Bhreascleit (Breascleit).

The best thing about a small community is that everybody knows everything about you. They have your back. The worst thing is that everbody knows everything about you. They're on your back.

My mother talks with Iain Bhreascleit. The conversation is pan-generational and includes dozens of people in a vast network that spans sea and land.

"...she was at the counter in Woollies when Peggy-Ann a' Phomman was there."

"That's right, Peggy's brother was a warper at Sticky's Mill and then went to Inverness when Chrissie got the job in the Station Hotel. They were engaged at the time but she met someone from Fraserburgh so then he came home."

"That's when he met Alice. I was at the dance when I first saw them together. Did Joan ever marry?"

"Yes, remember Murdo G, whose uncle had the shop? It was to a friend of his who came home with him when he was doing his National Service."

"I remember him. From Dewesbury. A joiner to trade. They moved to Perth after the wedding. They've got two boys and a girl. They were home a few years ago. I saw them in Murdo Maclean's. The girl is so like her mother. I could see the Carloway side in her. She went into nursing."

"Of course, Murdo G was with John the Scone on the Loch Seaforth for a while, too."

"It's a shame what happened to John."

"It is. They say drink is a good friend…"

"…but a bad master. Well, at least he's good-living now."

"Better late than never. He was lucky he met Màiri Plastic when he did. It's probably why he's still with us. But such a waste. He was clever… He could have done anything he wanted, John."

"There's so much tragedy in the world."

"It's full of it…"

Genealogy is indeed a deep and wide blood river with many tributaries and a huge delta. Ever-moving and permanent it runs through people's heads.

I'm reading the paper and half-watching the opening ceremony of the 1990 Commonwealth Games in Auckland. The city's mayor, a woman, is making a speech. "That's your cousin," says Uncle Kenneth. "Who? Her? On the TV?!" I say. "Yes," he says. "She was here visiting a few years ago."

She is (now) Dame Catherine Tizard (née Maclean), former Governor General of New Zealand, whose parents emigrated there in 1933 and is related on my father's side.

The day Donald Trump is inaugurated as US President, his first cousin is seen coming out of Tesco in Stornoway wearing a boiler suit and carrying a plastic bag.

My grandfather on my mother's side was called the Brùnach and he lived with us until his death in 1964. By then he was blind. His legendary gift was that he knew every sheep earmark on the island. Hundreds of them. These *comharradh*, like a cattle brand, were unique to each household and comprised a kind of visual code of slices, cuts and holes on the left and right ears. Our family *comharradh* was *bàrr taisgeal dà bheum foidhpe agus slisinn os cionn a chluais dheas*. There's a kind of poetic metre to it, which doesn't translate. (Two cuts below the dressed left tip and a slice at the top of the right ear. I think.)

The yarns about his extraordinary mental recall were legion. They once got lost crossing the moor. So the Brùnach caught a sheep, felt its ear in the dark and was able to ascertain their position.

He was in The Neptune with a friend who got talking to someone at the bar. "Do you know this fellow?" he asked the Brùnach. "No," he said. And then, "*Dè an comharradh a th'agaibh?*" (What earmark do you have?) When told, he said, "Well, that's an Uig earmark." From which he was able to tell, not just who the person was but who his relatives were. Uig is over forty miles away from Coll.

Because how you were identified was never in the interrogative – "What's your name?" or "Where are you from?" – but "*Cò leis thu?*" (Who do you belong to?) Or, in this instance, "Who are your sheep?"

So many extraordinary ordinary people. Folk wisdom in abundance. The Ruiseanach (The Russian) – nobody knows why he was called that – was born an old man, a simple soul, often teased but treated with great fondness by all. One time in my auntie's house he heard that a young man in the village was getting married and said, scornfully, "*Chan eil an airgead aig an fhear ud a chuireadh còta mòr air glaisean.*" (That guy doesn't have the money to put an overcoat on a sparrow.)

Crofting was crofting. A portfolio of work that, alongside another job, comprised a living: fishing, owning sheep or livestock (cattle, chickens), planting potatoes and vegetables, cutting peats for fuel, Harris Tweed – the villages rang with the *shickety-shick shickety-shick* of Hattersley looms in weaving sheds.

Gardens were mostly backdoor allotments. There wasn't a lawnmower in the entire district and if grass was cut at all, it was with a scythe for hay. As kids, when the nights drew in, gang raids on these patches for turnips and carrots was a favourite adventure.

A vegetable heist. Writing this, the thrill of munching into a raw turnip fills my nostrils.

Oidhche Shamhna – Halloween – was the creative zenith of the year. There's something exhilarating about dressing up in old, ill-fitting, mismatched clothes, especially the access and anonymity it gave you. Masks were fashioned from off-cuts of linoleum or you wore one of the shop-bought papier-mâché ones. As the night wore on the mouth area became saliva soggy. That distinctive smell is rooted in the soil of my brain.

Collection areas to "run" were canvassed over successive nights as if in a political campaign – the Poileagan, Outend Coll, Inner Coll, Brevig, Vatisker. In house after house, unmasked, you were of course identified through your parentage and lineage: "*Tha e cho coltach ri athair!*" (He's so like his father!) Eventually, after several nights, there was enough in the coffers for a big party. With Jaffa Cakes.

It was followed by Guy Fawkes Night, which had been preceded by weeks of scavenging rubbish for the great bonfire on the *mullach* (a raised area above the village). The most prized fuel was car tyres. From the hill you could see fires blazing in all the villages, Outend Coll, Back, Point, Laxdale, Tong, Melbost... No adults were ever present near these huge open-air furnaces. It was just something for the kids.

There were no pavements, no streetlights and you found your way about at night with a torch. Our beloved sheepdog, Ben, was killed by a lorry on the way to a bonfire, his body whirling under the wheels as if in a tumble dryer. Our next dog was called Cocoa, an unlovable, short-haired ginger mongrel. He resembled a roll of ham on four legs and barked at his own shadow, fought with every dog in the village and was indestructible. The milkman stopped one day to say that he was sorry but he had killed our dog and had brought the body back. When he opened the back of the van, Cocoa fell out, limped lumpily along the path, wobbled into the house, skidding on the lino, somehow clambered upstairs and went under a bed, where he whined miserably. My Uncle Seonaidh demanded of my mother that he be allowed to put the poor animal out of its misery, that it was sheer cruelty. But she couldn't face it. Next day, Cocoa was back. Barking at everything and nothing. He lived till he was twenty-one years old, supporting my theory that the less you care about some things the better off they are – and the better off you are.

Highland and Islands hospitality is renowned. It's a shame the weather is not so accommodating. Especially most of the year. Maybe our generosity is a form of compensation.

We don't have double-glazing and during the frequent winter gales the sash windows rattle like a milk-float down a cobbled street. Basins and towels are laid along the sills to collect and soak up the rainwater. The house has no insulation. Solid, poured-concrete walls are highly effective at conducting the cold and damp directly into the interior. The only heat source is the peat fire in the living room and all summer we are enslaved to peat-cutting to feed it over the long winter. Every house on every croft in every village is shadowed with a long peat-stack out the back: a carefully constructed, herring-boned, architectural feature.

In the autumn, earwigs find their way into corners and crannies of the house, sometimes into your bed. Crabby, summer-fattened spiders bounce in their webs outside, and on warm evenings huge bomber moths thud against the window panes.

The earlier houses, the *taighean dubh*, the "black" – or, more correctly, *taighean-tughadh*, thatched houses – had double stone walls around a core of earth, a dense insulated roof and deeply recessed windows. Squat, hunkered, limpet houses, glued to the land. Of the land. Impervious to bad weather. The cradle of the *cèilidh*. An acquaintance who was born and lived his first six years in a black house, recalls that he had never experienced cold such as when they moved to their newly built "white" house on the croft.

Our cats sleep on top of the telly for warmth and under the copper hot water tank in the cupboard beside the fire. My hamster, Harry, dies of hypothermia in his tin box under my bed. I remember his cold little body, curled in my hand. Ordered by post, he had come all the way from Inverness – perhaps originally from Syria or Siberia – arriving one dark night on the ferry. For this.

I always imagined him having had a little suitcase.

He'd already had a narrow squeak. One night my mother went out to the peat-stack with the torch when she heard a *whirrrr-rrrrr whirrrrrrrrrr* in the darkness. The torch revealed Harry, surrounded by a ring of cats, eyes glowing. She put him in her pocket.

On Sunday night, there is enough hot water for the weekly bath. The peaty water a dark amber, the colour of strong tea. No duvets. Bedding is a *cuibhrig* – a densely woven, heavy wool blanket – in multiple layers. It's an effort to breathe under the weight. Essential at bedtime is a hot water bottle. A piggy. This could either be a stoneware bottle, flattened along one side with a stopper in the middle, or a modern one made of ribbed rubber.

Now, picture the stretched, bleached-white beaches; lush green machair freckled with flowers; the blasted, russet moor; the houses huddled in villages or strung out along the road. The epic, pristine landscape seasoned and garnished with abandoned, rusting cars.

On Lewis, a brand new British model like a Morris Marina or an Austin Allegro has a lifespan of about six months before it is shot-blasted with rust. Nothing survives the island salt-bath.

Once a car reaches the end of its allotted span, it is driven to a final resting place in the hinterland. Not that anyone much cares where it was dumped. Plain sight is still out of mind. Doesn't matter, you can't eat scenery. Dead buses, towed to the moor are used as tea-sheds and for shelter when at the peats. The ginger junk is everywhere.

In 2009's *The Isle of Rust*, inspired by the island's signature material, corrugated iron, Jonathan Meades sums up Lewis thus: "This thrilling environment is created by a complete disregard for that most sacred of cows, *the* environment." (My italics)

What Meades films though is a more cleaned-up island. Dumping is now illegal. A response by the newly formed Comhairle nan Eilean (Western Isles Council, d.o.b. 1974) to the letters from tourists that appeared seasonally in the *Stornoway Gazette*. Each a version of "We visited your beautiful island where the people are so open, warm and friendly. Such a pity that it is blighted/blemished/disfigured, etc, by the wanton abandonment of scrap cars."

Where are we now? What day is it? What time? Saturday night in Stornoway. Closing time. Chips. We meander past the Town Hall *en route* to the last bus home. A set of concrete steps leads to an open door at the top and onto the back of the stage. Through it drifts the pedal steel strains of Country & Western star Boxcar Willie, from Texas, singing his melancholy, hard luck, hard life hobo stories to a full house.

He's kin. He's at home here. He belongs. Even if the nearest rail-road is on the other side of the country in Inverness. Or a six-hour sea trip away at Kyle of Lochalsh.

Part II

The Infernal City

Peter Capaldi with John Rogan, 'Bastards from Hell' gig,
February 1978, Glasgow School of Art

Born out of Wedlock

Some weeks into my first term at Glasgow School of Art I saw a notice inviting would-be actors to take part in a theatre production of *Frankenstein*. I went along to try and meet people. To be sociable. To make an effort.

It's where I met Peter Capaldi. In one of the tenements on Renfrew Street requisitioned by the art school for a department. A compelling, gregarious figure in a long dark coat and trailing scarf, he was going to be the leading man.

The project's mastermind was Iain McCaig, who, like Peter, was in the Graphics department. Brought up in Canada but originally and spiritually Californian, he was a bit of a misfit in Graphics. His extraordinary illustrations of elves, aliens, dragons and monsters were admired but unfashionable. He would be fully vindicated when he went to work for George Lucas as a conceptual designer, famously on the *Star Wars* prequel *The Phantom Menace*.

But that was back in the future.

Iain had grandiose ideas for the play, involving vast stage sets with rising platforms and special effects. He was ruthlessly positive, and when he spoke, we could see it; the dry ice, the Creature flared by lightning.

One day, he announced that there was going to be a fundraising concert for the production. And we would form a band.

I was recruited, with my basic skill set and the plexiglass guitar I'd bought in Aberdeen. Peter was to be the front man. Iain would be the drummer, and John Rogan from Glasgow's East End was brought in on bass.

In this Year Zero nobody was any better than anyone else. It was all potential. Even so, the fact that Peter Capaldi was cast as

Victor Frankenstein and I was Second Seaman was prophetic. We also serve who only stand and wait.

And wait we did. Save for the odd read-through, little happened on the dramatic front. The play became peripheral, vestigial. It withered in the shadow of its own monstrous ambition. Hard to say whether *Frankenstein* died or never came to life in the first place. At the end there were no notices, mourners or eulogies.

But the band lived on. We rehearsed in a basement in the Haldane building on Hill Street and our first gig was to be during Activities Week in February '78, when the art school staged events, film, happenings and the like.

To announce ourselves the band needed a name that, in the fashion of the time, not so much commanded attention, as rugby-tackled it. "The Bastards from Hell" was that name. A kind of infantile raspberry. I thought that people would get it, snigger and forget it. But no. It has been as hard to remove from the public record as chewing gum from your pubic hair.

The gig was riotous: a sweaty, beer-soaked, bawls-out, cacophonous free-for-all, devoid of much musical merit but utterly exhilarating. The setlist was a dog's dinner of covers, culminating with John bawling out *Pretty Vacant*. Were it not so unpretentious and lustily enjoyable, it might have been considered an art happening.

The Bastards only played once. An incandescent meteorite flaring briefly, luminously, across an unnoticed corner of the night sky. From now on, though, we needed to get serious and rebrand. So we chose an even worse name – as bad, in fact, as "The Beatles".

I think there was some kind of blind spot. That there were allusions to surrealism. Or film. I'm sure we toyed with the name "The Dream Sequence". Or that we thought we were being ironic. Maybe, but by the time we'd gone public it was too late. The caterpillar that was "The Bastards from Hell" had metamorphosed into

"The Dreamboys".

Now it's the name of a male strip group. Not that I mind being associated, however fraudulently, with oiled abs.

Outsiders

Despite its prestige, Glasgow School of Art didn't have a recip-rocal agreement with the universities and we couldn't get in to other student unions. We had to loiter outside, forlornly asking members to sign for us at the door. It underscored the feeling of being an outsider, even in the "Further Education Community".

But we did get in. Through the backdoor. We got a gig at the Queen Margaret Union at Glasgow University on Sunday night, the 2nd of February, 1979. It was an upstairs lounge bar. Carpeted.

This performance, too, achieved a kind of notoriety. There were complaints about the volume and it became a face-off and a race as to whether we could get to the end of the set before the power was turned off.

Some in the audience had huge admiration for our stance. By then, attitude was beginning to have a premium beyond compe-tence. It's what elevated the performance. Made it feel somehow significant and authentic. Two gigs in and we were getting a reputation.

Musically, we were progressing. Sartorially, some of us weren't keeping up. John's wardrobe was cheesecloth shirts and patched, flared denim jeans. Whereas my kit was usually selectively sourced from Oxfam. And soon, the tensions within the band were as tight as a tourniquet. Round our jugular. It ended, like a teenage rela-tionship, with a petty squabble during a bitchy rehearsal. And John was gone. No hard feelings. We reverted to being mates.

Our new bassist was Temple Clark. I'd not heard of anyone before or since named after a building or a part of the cranium. But it suited him. He was from the New Town in Edinburgh and his dad was a producer at the BBC. He had a younger sister called

Stroma, which is also the name of an island.

Despite all his annoying advantages – over six feet tall, lean, clever, talented, well-off and handsome – I never resented or disliked him. Michael Palin's wife is supposed to have said, "Honestly, Michael, if you get any nicer, I shall have to divorce you." A bit like that.

One day he told me, "I've bought a wok." How can you buy a walk? "It's a pan for Chinese cooking." All part of my ancillary education. I wouldn't go so far as to call it the University of Life, though.

One of our first original songs, *Bela Lugosi's Birthday*, was a rare collaborative effort Peter and I wrote, with an ambiguous creepy lyric:

I'm out and seeing the sights again
Sliding through another day
Looking for another place to stay,
In the alleys after dark
Slipping in and moving fast
That's my way,
All the people in all of their houses
Asleep, tonight,
They can't see me
And they can't hear me
Close their eyes

We performed it for the first time at Glasgow College of Technology on the 20th of October, 1979. That gig was immortalised in our first ever review in the *NME*, which focused on our "flailing din" and described me as looking "about twelve" and with the "permanent aspect of a kitchen scullion". Peter, meanwhile, was the band's "main asset".

Still, at least it finished on a positive note: "Despite the frequently unlistenable shambles, it did improve. Three songs were promising and funny. Towards the end, lots of us were smiling. That must be worth something."

It wasn't the first review we had. That was in a fanzine called *Sanity is Boring*, which was a handful of photocopied pages paperclipped together. There were no photographs but it was more advanced than some, in that it was typed. And who's to say that the reviewer didn't go on to a career with the *New York Times*. Here's why:

> Some people have to say you have to look right to succeed in rock. In that case the Dream Boys are doomed to fail. The guitarist looked a real Mummies boy... Apart from their diabolical name the band played some good, some bad songs and a couple of excellent songs. They started with a fast one but the ones after that were slower...

Day of Shame was more sophisticated in that it was stapled and carried pictures, although that was offset by being handwritten, albeit very neatly:

> The Dreamboys are an amazing mob from Glasgow who bound with energy, the guitarist looks like a cross between a Gorbals Diehard and Jimmy Clitheroe – who says they sound like the Cramps?

I didn't understand these references. On the page, they inset a mugshot of a five-year-old kid with the caption "A Dreamboy Impersonator".

Fumes 4 was typed, stapled, photocopied AND had photographs, so that's a full house right there. I'm not bothering putting (sic) after anything. Verbatim:

> the dreamboys at the doune castle, you would no doubt have a
> think after that, because the boys don't usually play this type of
> venue .. why because they are a class band.
>
> So why did they play .. it was simply that NEWSPEAK WERE
> supposed to play that night but could not owing to their drum-
> mer acquiring glandular fever. so the boys were phoned at
> the last minute to fill in the vacancy, the reason why the three
> quarter full dungeon almost practically emptied, no-one was
> expecting the dreamboys to play that night.. The boys made the
> best of a bad thing. starting of with outer limits, the newspeak
> fans listened, was it the musical night they were expecting --- i
> dont know but by the end a fair percentage of them had gone..
> the twenty or so that remained I can only assume were fans in
> for an unexpected treat ..
>
> the band done two enjoyable sets ... if you have not seen them
> yet get to the next gig ... you should not be dissapointed......

God, how young and innocent and enthusiastic it was. I could
imagine them in their tower blocks with their Letraset and scissors and glue, waiting for their photographs to be developed at
Boots. Going into a print shop with their dole money and asking
for fifty copies, or getting their sister to do it on the fly at the office.
Then the finished editions being dropped off at the record shops,
ready to hit the streets. EXTRA EXTRA...

Dear Green (and Blue) Place

Late Seventies Glasgow had a feral energy, fuelled by a hi-octane mix of gallusness, garrulousness, black backlash humour, red politics and DIY creativity. With a pinch of violence as an accelerant. It was the antidote to Aberdeen. I was cured.

"Glasgow's Miles Better", the Garden Festival, European City of Culture: the council's campaigns to renovate their theatre of urban decay hadn't yet begun. Merchant City was not so much a no-go zone as a no-point-in-going zone. It wasn't until Café Gandolfi opened there in 1979, presumably because of preferential property and business rates, that it began its journey to gentrification. Probably something's been lost along the way, but I can't think what. The Saracen's Head pub (The Sarry Heid) is still there.

I got beaten up in Finnieston by a bunch of neds as we passed a newsagents one Sunday night. I'd offended them by wearing straight-leg cord trousers and a jacket from Oxfam. Standard-grade abuse and then they came swarming after me.

Under such circumstances, best practice was to curl into a ball and cover your head so they can't do as much damage. They were usually quite content, fulfilled even, as long as they were booting the shit out of you.

I careered into the middle of Argyle Street, went down, curled and covered, and they only stopped smiting me when the traffic backed up. As beaten and scrambled as an egg, but, aside from multiple boot-marks and bruises, unharmed. Went for a pint.

Now the area is all Crabshakk and swank.

Not so lucky was Dole, who was studying at the Nautical College across the river. Always entertaining company with endless yarns, especially of hard-luck stories with women. Alas, the hardest luck story of all was still ahead of him: That would be the day he met his wife.

One night midweek, Peter, Temple, Dole and I were walking up Renfield Street. On our left further up, opposite the Odeon Cinema, was the Targets Bar. It had a cross-hair logo across the front and bouncers in suits at the door.

There was a tangible sense of menace when a couple of customers drifted across the pavement from the entrance. But Peter and I passed without incident. Then, a commotion behind and Dole was down in a puddle of blood. He had been booted in the face. The doors of the bar opened and a full crew came streaming out and went for us. We scattered. The bouncers leaned against the wall with a bored expression.

After the local youth had had their kicks, so to speak, we took Dole to the Royal Infirmary. Badly concussed, his head swelled out like a pumpkin and he needed stitches. The following day he couldn't sit his end-of-term exams and, as a result, left the Nautical College at the end of the year. We will never know as to whether the doing he got that night was ultimately a good or a bad thing.

The most popular wines in Glasgow were Eldorado, Lanliq and Queen Anne: cheap fortified plonque usually shipped over as a jelly and bottled on site. Pubs in Port Glasgow and Greenock would have trays of glasses prepped before they opened in the morning. And Buckfast. The consistent market leader.

There *were* wine bars. For instance, a shack called Dick's Wine Bar in the barely lit Ripper-like back streets of Finnieston. Assuredly, however, a sauvignon-free zone.

Neither should we forget what an uptight, reactionary city Glasgow was. Monty Python's *The Life of Brian* was banned. There was a ferocious "stop this filth" campaign in the West End against some hapless newsagent who wanted to sell top-shelf magazines like *Penthouse* and *Men Only*.

Shortly before he was permanently released, I saw convicted murderer Jimmy Boyle – a reminder of razor-city, gangland Glasgow – with his minder in the city centre, on day-release from the special unit in Barlinnie. Not long after his autobiography, *A Sense of Freedom*, had been dramatised for TV. Like me, he was now studying sculpture.

Flashback: when Rangers visited Aberdeen in 1974, it felt like eleventh-century Viking marauders had arrived. Shops on the thoroughfare to Pittodrie were either boarded up or trashed. Rampant inebriation... yes, Virginia, it was totally mental (as Glasgow vernacular would have it). The match was stopped because of a pitch invasion and the city centre was on lockdown until the late train that night. Without a fatality it wasn't even news. Final score was 2-1 Rangers. Weeks later we were in the Celtic end for a mid-week fixture. Same. Different colour scheme. Carry-outs and piss running down the terraces. That was Glasgow "on tour" in the 1970s.

Now it's a UNESCO City of Music. Then there was the Burns Howff, the Amphora on Sauchiehall Street, and little else. Breeding grounds for blues-rocky outfits, with names like "Sneaky Pete" and "Bite the Pillow", who had survived the Sixties. There was a whiff of hard-men and pints-of-heavy and a-bit-of-blow and working-class heroism, all wrapped up in leather, denim and cheesecloth. Much was made of musicianship of the endless noo-dling guitar solo kind.

The Mars Bar was a sticky carpet dive that had to change its name on account of copyright infringement of the yet-to-be-deep-fried confection of the same name. It became the Countdown and we found our way there, as did earlier frontrunners Simple Minds. Called "Johnny & the Self-Abusers" before they renounced their status as self-declared wankers.The dearth of gig-space was apparently due to a local Victorian or Edwardian era bye-law. A hangover from the days of music hall. Pubs were barred from putting on entertainment because it would be competition for the music halls and theatres. A kind of closed shop from a bygone age. As a comedian you hadn't lived unless you'd died in Glasgow.

But as it says in *Jurassic Park*, "life always finds a way", even if it means jumping the species barrier by going to Paisley. It's hard to believe that a pub in Paisley called the Bungalow was a one-time West of Scotland version of CBGBs. Yet, at the time, almost every Scottish band that made it – and the majority, including us, that didn't – appeared there.

Blackout

We played at the Bungalow on a riotous Christmas Eve. Afterwards, we drove to my flat in the West End before heading to Bishopbriggs to spend Christmas Day at Peter's house.

Next morning, it was evident something was amiss. Peter couldn't open his eyes. He could barely see. His vertical hairstyle had been sustained by gel, which, activated by sweat, had run into his eyes during the gig and sort of *set* overnight. Ahead of us was a walk of a couple of miles into Buchanan Street bus station and I led him like Blind Pew through the snowy, deserted Glasgow streets.

It didn't get better and after an hour or so at the house, with Christmas dinner on ice, so to speak, there was nothing for it but A&E. The scene there was like a sitcom scripted by Rab C. Hogarth. Drunks with bandaged hands, skewered while carving the turkey. Aside from the staff, I think we were the only sober people there.

Peter spent an hour under an eye bath while his Dad and I waited in this curious Crimbo-limbo. When we got home he spent the rest of the day lying in a darkened room. I don't remember anything else; maybe I've blacked it out.

Another time, *The Ten Commandments* fanzine reported: "Following a sore stomach during their last Paisley appearance Dreamboys' vocalist Peter Capaldi was forced to rush off stage mid-song and empty his earlier consumed fish supper in the gents. But all was well, he returned in time to finish the number."

Domain of the Sun God

The Apollo theatre was a Glasgow institution, which has since been wiped off the map, demolished and replaced by a multi-screen cinema. But the name survives as a brand of window blinds – an Icarus-like plunge in status.

It was a ten-minute walk from the art school and the default venue for every touring band that came to Glasgow, from the rising New Wave punk scene to the then superstars.

The Apollo was a large yet intimate venue with stalls, boxes, balcony and gods. Who did I see there? Dr Feelgood, Stiff Little Fingers, The Ramones, The Clash supported by Richard Hell and the Voidoids, The Jam, Blue Oyster Cult, The Buzzcocks, The Stranglers, Joy Division, Mink De Ville, Alex Harvey, Elvis Costello, Darts, Ian Dury and the Blockheads (and the whole Stiff Records roster, Nick Lowe *et al*), Iggy Pop, The Who and – twice in a week – David Bowie.

I was in the gods on Bowie's last night and the balcony was bouncing like a trampoline. When Status Quo played, you really ought to have been strapped in. It was all too easy to imagine the be-denimed bodies pinging like popcorn through the air to the stalls far below.

The Who were a band from a mythical age when gods threw lightning bolts at each other from mountain tops. It was a huge event. To get tickets, we needed to queue all night. Sleeping bags. Relieving ourselves in back alleys. There was a contingent coming down from Lewis that included John A, who was a fisherman. The usual routine was: get on the boat back of midnight on Sunday and work flat-out until landing the catch on Thursday night. Hit the bar. Friday, get the ship into shape. Hit the bar. Saturday, get the sheep into shape. Hit the bar. Dry out on Sunday, then back on the boat again. So my abiding memory of the concert was of John snoring his way through the entire set while the loudest band on the planet crashed and windmilled away in front of him.

Calum's father was a butcher and each time someone from Lewis went to Glasgow, they were given a carrier bag of fresh meat to feed their son. This time, on arrival, it was put behind the bar at His Nibs. The bag though was not recovered until several days later and by then contained several pounds of rotting flesh, which was dumped on the way home.

Postcard from the Past

The "Postcard Revolution" – a.k.a. "The Sound of Young Scotland" – superimposed a bunch of self-consciously boyish bands with floppy fringes and check shirts against a scratchy, skinny soundtrack of vintage guitars, such as Epiphone Filibusters and Gretsch Breadboards.

Their graphics plundered post-war shortbread-tin Scotland for maximum Caledonian waggery. The movement was spearheaded by a B-side Andy Warhol called Alan Horne – a right wee Svengali, so he wis. The mirror image in Edinburgh was Fast Records. The collective noun might have been a "snobbery".

History is written not just by the winners, but for and about the winners. So now, officially, Postcard Records is all that happened. We were just aggregate. Filler and fodder, useful only as an unfavourable comparison. In theory, we might as well have never existed. If we did, it was off the record.

But there *were* others. Urbanly alienated postnatal Gary Numan outfits and Joy Division long-coats, like Positive Noise. Teutonic Veneer was the handle for a peroxide character called Russell Barry, who it was said was in the Navy and spent half the year under the polar ice cap in a nuclear submarine. I needed that to be true. He performed behind huge expensive banks of electronic kit. A one-man band, only without the cymbals between his knees, big drum on his back and kazoo.

And the splendidly named Defiant Pose, who I never saw but envisaged as spikey-headed little urchins, scowling fiercely for the camera. Like Joan Eardley's Townhead kids, or *Oor Wullie*.

The Zones and Restricted Code were evidently influenced by traffic regulations.

In a category of his own was Jimmy, later of Fun Patrol and James King and the Lone Wolves. He began as Jimmy Loser & the Backstabbers. Jimmy had respect, serious musical chops and was the unvarnished real deal. Also bad glasses and dentures. In Glasgow, it doesn't get much more authentic than that.

The Cuban Heels were a roguish crew: a good, tough, tight band but perhaps not distinctive or fashionable enough to draw the right kind of attention in this human zoo. Too much R&B, instead of Velvet Underground, in their DNA. Like Olympic athletes, you have to choose your parents very carefully. Same goes for influences.

Laurie, their guitarist and songwriter, was from Greenock and would take the train home after rehearsals in the Krazy House on Argyll Street. One night his train stopped at Mount Florida and the carriage flooded with Rangers fans from a match at Hampden.

A Catholic, he could see it coming. "That a guitar ye've got there, mate? Gie's a song!" No fool, he chuckled knowingly and said, "Aye. It'll be *The Sash* ye're after," and proceeded to play and sing the only line he knew of the Protestant national anthem, *The Sash My Father Wore*. If they didn't join in, he was fucked.

"*Sure, I'm an Ulster Orangeman…*" He needn't have worried, they roared in like a jet engine and parted company on the best of terms. It was an interdenominational triumph, rare for those days. Just that nobody knew it.

The Recognitions were properly musical and even had a band uniform. They fuelled my inferiority complex with complex, off-beat, catchy songs with clever titles like *Singularly Gyrate*. I thought they were going to be huge. But they imploded. Next time I saw Paul-the-Singer, a gifted guitarist, he had become a gifted busker.

Given that we were that loathed, privileged thing – an Art School Band – I think we could legitimately have been accused of letting the side down. Our pretentiousness wasn't really up to scratch. Our influences were American gothic, sci-fi and B-movies, Hammer horror shoved through an influence filter from Bowie to the Velvet Underground and Wire. Even Dean Martin and, of course, Frank. Eventually, our schtick was christened "bizarro-pulp" in a review in *Sounds*. In due course, we would discover our lodestone, The Cramps.

Because we began as a drama project by-product, we were theatrical, only without props – frog masks, etc. With Peter upfront, though, every performance was a Performance, an Event, an Occasion.

Twenty-four Hours in the Back of a Box Van

I had never driven on the mainland before. Never been on a motorway or dual carriageway. And when I passed my driving test in Stornoway in 1976 there wasn't even a set of traffic lights in the town. The single small roundabout we called the doughnut, behind Goathill Road, was inadequate preparation for the elaborate junction boxes of Glasgow and its environs. But I was the only one in the band with a licence. By default, I was the driver.

So began the first instalment of paying our dues. The phrase implies a kind of hire-purchase on a future career and the steep creep up the learning curve until you've learned it and you've earned it.

The phone rang. We had a gig in London: our first Big Break. From the bottom of the bill we were to prop up a roster of bands at the Music Machine in Camden, among them Those French Girls, from Stirling – an all-male crew with a front man called Sean Something. They usually closed their set with a song called *It's Always Fucking Raining*. An astute observation, to be sure. Another was called *Regular Sex*. But that was a concept with which I was not familiar.

Normally a Transit would have sufficed but this time we needed a box van because we had to collect their equipment too. From Stirling. A round trip of a couple of hours from Glasgow before we could even head for London.

I had a summer job as a kitchen porter in Baird Hall near Charing Cross. It was a term-time residence for Strathclyde University students, but during the recess it was used as a hotel by SAGA. Social Amenities for the Golden Age. Holidays for Old People.

I had worked the early shift and in the late afternoon we set off round the city picking up gear and personnel. For once I was reprieved from driving. This time it would be a roadie called Big John, who had his girlfriend, Mae, upfront. There were six of us in the back. Steerage. All-in-it-together. Stinking inside the box. We lifted the sliding shutter door a few inches at the bottom for ventilation.

At Stirling, we got out, gulped some unused air, loaded up and then drove south through the night. A sprawl of bodies among the scatter of blankets, pillows, bags, instrument cases, amps and speakers.

It was before personal stereos. It was too dark to read. There was no view to indicate progress or calibrate distance. The tarmac blurred in the few-inch gap for hour after hour. Night fell. There were a couple of pit stops somewhere, I don't remember. I must have slept sometime. I don't remember. We must have talked a lot. I don't remember.

Eventually, since we got there, we must have arrived. It was not yet 6am. We had a whole day in London with nothing to do and nowhere to go. Nothing rhymes with nothing. We had no money; we might as well hang around Camden. Doing nothing.

Nobody in London seemed to realise – far less care – that *we had arrived*. The wilderness of that day.

At last. Back of five, we were able to get access to sound-check. But. Only after all the other bands on the bill. Another false summit, another mirage as the evening eked into night. Eventually, we were allocated five minutes, and plugged in and played. Everything was wrong. We couldn't hear each other and flailed and groped in the sonic murk. Then we were kicked off.

Where once there was too much time, now there was too little.

The warm-up hardly seemed worth it. Almost immediately our seminal moment arrived and at 9pm we were sent on stage. First on. Hello, London.

The Music Machine had "seen better days", in the same way a corpse can be described as having been "formerly alive". It was a shabby, cavernous dump where the carpets, pock-marked with fag-burns, felt like they had been marinated in glue. There were about seven people in the place. Upfront was a huge Buster Bloodvessel skinhead with full regulation boots 'n' braces, who kept shouting and spitting at us: Oi this and Oi that. The sound was a shambles. We might as well have been playing in separate rooms. All too soon and yet not soon enough, it was over.

And the night trundled on with its cargo of bands. I lay on the filthy floor in the dressing room and went into a coma. I got woken up with a violent shake. I had to get up. We had to shift the gear into the van. We had to drive up the road. I was shiveringly cold, sleep deprived, teetering with exhaustion. And my accommodation for a second night was but one step up from a cattle truck. The only positive was that I was physically incapable of staying awake.

Outside, obliviously, the road flickered by once more in the few-inch gap, until somewhere, beyond Birmingham, a change of rhythm and vibration suggested that we were pulling into a service station. We stopped and I heard people get out.

I was by now fully conscious. But I was also still asleep. With an escalating sense of panic I found I was paralysed. I couldn't even open my eyes. My soul thrashed but my body did not even twitch. Was I dead? It was an existential moment. Like waking up, nailed inside a coffin – in the back of a box van, abandoned in a motorway car park.

"Have you tried switching it off and on again?" All I could do was try and go back to "sleep" – lose consciousness – and pray that a neural reset and reboot would happen. And it did. After a fluttery, dysconscious, sputtering pseudo-sleep, my neurons realigned and I was awake and ambulant again, watching the tarmac through the few-inch gap.

On a muggy mid-morning we arrived back where we had started, in Glasgow. I got dropped off on Great Western Road and, as I negotiated my way through the clutter of people, I wondered if this is what it felt like to be one of the living dead.

Now I had to get ready for work. For the next eight hours I would need to be an imposter and go undercover as a functioning human being.

By lunchtime, I had clocked on and assumed my alter ego as a kitchen scullion, cleaning pans, dishing out dinners, mopping floors, running bets for the chefs at the bookie's across the road... Our journey seemed like a hallucination. A bad trip. But was this reality any better?

A black box flight recorder might have traced how aspiration had accelerated into delusion, and collided with the cliff face of reality. A news crew might have reported from the scene as our ambitions were cut from the wreckage, bodies like broken crash-test dummies, survivors hospitalised, the others sent to the morgue.

In another idiom, the great opportunity had been one step forward and three steps back. Down a flight of stairs. But in karma, how rich and abundant would be the payback on the experience? Beyond measure, you would think. And though I didn't know it then, fate had decreed a trip to Aberdeen further down the line. Bonus points for that.

A Guy Walks Out of a Bar

We were between drummers. Iain McCaig had better things to do and Robin Livesey had got the job. He was an apprentice electrician from Rutherglen. Nothing wrong except there was no chemistry and, inevitably, he got fed up and chucked it.

In the meantime, we had landed a top gig at the Rock Garden on Queen Street. By then, the city bye-laws had loosened up and we didn't have to go to, literally, ridiculous lengths out of town to play. It was a bar aimed at the younger market: students, fashion-conscious, female-friendly, music, wine, beer and spirits on the gantry, decent *live* music. Food! An outstanding French onion soup, for example.

We borrowed H2O's drummer, Kenny, who made a good fist of it for a stand-in. Played in football shorts. It was one of those nights when the set took off and levitated. When all the hours, money, hassle, discomfort, disappointment and sacrifice that got you there seemed like a small price. I remember a similar rush at a packed-out gig at the 100 Club in London. At the end, Peter made a thing of thanking Kenny and saying that we needed a permanent drummer and if anybody knew of any, to get in touch and you've been really brilliant and thanks and GOOD NIGHT!

And then down with the usual thump: hauling gear down the stairs, loading up and moving on. Closing time, the van had been parked round the block and we were sitting on a stack of amps on the pavement waiting for it, when a girl came out of the bar and said, "Craig's a really good drummer," referring to the guy she had in tow. Despite being drunk, he seemed convincing, talked about his kit. Sure, what's to lose? So we arranged an audition at the Hellfire Club. There was a drum kit already there, so all he had to bring were his sticks.

It did not go well. He was clearly nervous but we made allowances. We were patient too, but no, this was not working out. At all. What to do? We could go to the pub.

Which is where the real audition took place. Craig Ferguson (for it was he) was younger than us, maybe eighteen, and worked behind the counter at the post office in Cumbernauld.

We got on like a whisky distillery on fire, which made it such a damn shame that he wasn't up to scratch. But we couldn't seem to get around to telling him he was a non-starter. He knew himself that he hadn't made it but he was game. He kept on about the drums and the set-up. If only he'd had a chance to use his own kit...

We didn't have the heart to say no. Long story short, he turned up with his own Pearl kit and killed it, kicking off with a thunderous version of the Robert Gordon number *The Way I Walk*. You're hired. It was the beginning of a most uncommon, bespoke relationship. We were now in our final incarnation.

Years later, I got a text telling me that I'm in the *Daily Mail*. The first of a number of impromptu appearances after Harry Papadopoulos's book of photographs came out. It was a photo from a gig we had done in the Third Eye Arts Centre. What made it news was that it was a before-they-were-famous shot of Peter Capaldi with Craig Ferguson on drums in the background. Temple and I were just spear-carriers. The Unmentionables.

Only it *isn't* Craig. It's Robin. It's indistinct enough to assume it is Craig. But it's not. So even though he's not there, he's there. While I'm there, but not. There must be a moral in there somewhere.

The Hellfire Club

David Henderson's Hellfire Club studio was on the ground floor of a tenement near Charing Cross. It was where we perpetrated most of our recordings. David was a very tall, spindly, gently spoken mixing desk sorcerer who with his sister Jaine had served his time with Simple Minds. On account of his look and demeanour, Peter had invented a medieval alter ego for him: The Shoe Lender. "Prithee, Shoe Lender, wilt thou not lend me a pair of thy fine leather brogues for my pilgrimage, I beseech thee?"

The Hellfire Club was our bunker. A hang-out, rehearsal space, retreat, fulcrum, epicentre. We spent as much time there as at the art school and only slightly less than the pub. There was something subterranean about it that seeped into the bones of the music.

Up-tech studios like CaVa were sonic labs with facilities to bring out what you had brought in. The Hellfire Club was more like an apothecary's or a medieval kitchen, with hares and pheasants hanging from the ceiling, potions racked up along the walls. Alchemy. Magic more than science.

It was where we recorded *Bela Lugosi's Birthday*, which we released on our own independent label, St Vitus Records. Borrowed the money from Peter's dad. Saint Vitus is the patron saint of dancers, young people... and dogs. And St Vitus's dance was a neurological disease common in the Middle Ages where victims danced themselves to death. John Peel played the single a couple of times, one time saying, "Oh yes, lambent and meticulous," which sent us scurrying for a dictionary to find out what "lambent" meant.

I was on the cover, supposedly a broken-hearted vampire at a late-night neon bar. Peter had sourced some morticians' wax and my ears were pointed up. Temple, with Kubrick-like attention to detail, even wrote a "Dear Bela" letter, which I had crushed in one hand, a large bourbon in the other.

The image was more elfin or goblin-like than one of the un-dead though. Craig referred to it as "The Leprechaun of Death".

The B-side was called *Outer Limits*. The song was like an episode of the eponymous TV programme, which, like *The Twilight Zone*, was cult viewing. Futuristic fables, morality tales with a knife twist.

It told a story: a couple meet at a Halloween party, but maybe she isn't really dressed up. *Maybe* she's in her normal attire, her ordinary work clothes.

We met in fancy dress, that's how it was to be
But I never learned to cope with all your idiosyncrasies
And in the cold light of the day things don't always look the same
I wondered were you really ill or did you always look that way?

It was in the Outer Limits
It was oh, such a long, long time ago
I was so happy, happy in the Outer Limits,
I never wanted to go

What she collected in glass jars was her affair, not mine
And how she spent all of her evenings and the rest of her spare
*   time,*
Her strange habits and strange hobbies made strange noises in
*   the night*
Oh, I guess I knew all along, something wasn't right

CHORUS

I asked her if she'd change her ways, she wouldn't even try
But I always used to tell her, I was just a normal guy
And when they caught her and they questioned me, well I had
   to testify
But like I always used to tell her, I'm just a regular guy

CHORUS

Oh no please don't take me away, n-o-o-o-o
I didn't know what she was; I didn't know who she was
I only loved her.

The coda was an extraordinary, deranged improvisation by Peter live in the studio. It sounds as though he's being hauled out of there in a straitjacket, screaming. It suggests betrayal is what normal guys do. Or maybe he's the crazy one.

A Gig at Random

Random isn't a club. It's just chance. I thought I'd pick one out of the memory basket and re-live it. A sentimental journey. How about The Apollo Lounge Bar in the centre of Glenrothes in Fife, on a Monday night? Despite Christianity and the Reformation, the ancient Greek Sun God remained popular in Scotland.

Bunking off art school at lunchtime, picking up the van, then the guys, the long drive across Scotland and the eventual entry into a dog-eared concrete town centre where silence reigned. It was one of those new towns that once supported a now extinct electronics industry. The kind where every shop, facility, amenity is tied into a concrete knot in the middle while the semis and council houses and schemes wander off aimlessly.

It wasn't the Music Machine, with its epic awfulness, annihilation of expectation and psychological ruin. It was more workaday, more benign, more domestic and therefore more representative of the day job.

The carpets were not so adhesive. The place was much smaller. There were probably eight to ten people there – men with pints, so it felt busier. They were sitting at tables so it was more "cabaret". There was no aggro, intimidation or for that matter, interest. A smattering of applause.

This was a Bar that had been lowered to our expectations.

The Christmas Tree

Unlike the Apollo Lounge, which was a one-off, we played the International Hotel, Grangemouth in East Stirlingshire, a few times. It was a typical, stone-built country house hotel with a small podium and dance floor at its centre. The natural habitat for Country & Western bands, show bands, wedding bands, Sydney Devine derivatives.

Why we, and others of our ilk, ended up there had something to do with the manager. He was called Guthrie and his younger brother Robin was in a band.

We always enjoyed the hospitality as much as a vague sense of being appreciated. But hardly anybody ever came. Of those that did, the most eye-catching and distinctive was a round-faced, young girl. She was always dressed up in an outlandish costume of her own devising that erred just the right side of fancy dress.

On account of her decorative nature she'd been dubbed "The Christmas Tree". Each time we played she came along and whirled unselfconsciously around the empty dance floor. I say it's not the number of fans you have, it's the quality.

Her name was Elizabeth Fraser and she was the singer in Robin Guthrie's band. We let them support us at the Bungalow bar; I can't say for sure if it was their first ever live gig.

The review of that gig in *Sounds* described Liz Fraser's "yelps grating against the scrapings of the two musicians who flank her, the whole underpinned by the bumpity-bump of a drum machine. 'The Cocteau Twins from Grangemouth' somebody whispers. It hardly seems to matter that there are three of them."

All Those Moments Will Be Lost in Time, Like Tears in Rain

Late in the day
Late in the year
Lately I've been
Having very bad dreams
Home Before Dark

It was a Thursday towards the end of the year and we were scheduled for band practice at the Hellfire Club after art school. It was already dark, bone cold and the rain was thrashing the streets. Taxi weather, if you could afford it. I turned up but, for whatever reason, nobody else did.

So I needed to re-orientate and do something else with this unexpected, unexplained night off. Somewhere out of this shite weather. First stop was the Griffin. Which is where I clocked Crockett. In the snug. He'd just left school and was a regular at our gigs. Often helped out as a roadie. Came from an anonymous suburb called Clarkston. I'd never been there.

After a couple of pints, he said we should get a bottle of whisky and go back to my flat. It was an outrageous, perhaps perilous idea. The hard stuff wasn't our drug of choice. Big medicine. But as we tend to say in the aftermath of a self-inflicted disaster, it seemed like a good idea at the time. Maybe, as a carry-out, it was just more portable than a ton of cans. Anyway, we did it and trudged up the long road. Half an hour later we were sitting on my bed passing the bottle. Talking.

Later, Crockett said, "Have you still got those mushrooms?"

Just in case you think I am about to make an omelette, some

context is required: a week or two earlier a fellow traveller called Max, in return for some slight favour, had gifted me an Embassy Regal fag packet stuffed with magic mushrooms. I just shoved it in my top drawer. Chances were it was going to get binned.

In the autumn, the cognoscenti harvested the nipple-headed little fungi in fields and on golf courses. I'd heard of one pilgrim who entered a field where there was a good crop. He spent a happy hour or so there, browsing and grazing, until he became aware, somewhere behind him, of a huge, black, ominous, snorting presence. A bull. He sprinted as if his feet had sprouted wings and flung himself over a barbed wire fence into a gorse thicket. Gasping like a decked fish, scraped raw but at least safe, he looked back into the field. It was a bin-liner.

So this wasn't our drug of choice either, but for the second time that night, here we were choosing it. The questionable decisions were stacking up.

We took a small handful each and waited. Nothing happened. Crockett said, "Give me the rest of these things." So we finished what was there. Then it started happening. Crockett said, with some urgency, "I need to see Tracy," his new squeeze who lived only a couple of blocks away. Why this should occur to him now was unclear. If he was that keen, he could have seen her hours ago instead of coming to my flat.

Because it was past midnight by now and I really did not want to go traipsing round the freezing streets on a plotline detour in the pissing rain. But I had to.

And to my surprise, I began to have a great time. The lights on the wet, glistening streets made it feel like being inside a giant chandelier. All the parked cars had Disneyesque personalities. Hilariously, a cheeky wee red sports car kept nudging the rear end of a pissed-off white Transit van.

Crockett, though, was marching ahead with serious intent and

I could barely keep up. When we got there, it turned out Tracy wasn't in.

So we headed for The Wee C's flat on Woodlands Road. And luckily he *was* in. Also there was his pal Custard, an ample Black guy in a safari jacket, who was skinning up. We sat chatting, listening to reggae in the warm kitchen, gently steaming by the gas fire. It was like being on a lush, illuminated tropical island in this dark urban ocean. And then, in minutes, Crockett got up. We had to go again. Chasing the small hours while the black sky drained its contents on us.

When I caught up with him I saw that he had tears streaming down his face and I realised I had to be a grown-up. I said, "Come on, Croc, let's head back. Cup of tea. It's been a long night."

Crockett still lived at home with his folks. Under fairly strict house rules. His dad was a cop. We were all kids but he was even more of a kid than we were, so you could argue that we had a duty of care. Chances are his parents felt it was safe for him to regularly overnight it with us in Glasgow. We were older, responsible, respectable boys from good homes in further education. We'd look after him. And I'm confident that if I'd said in my defence that he had scripted and directed this bleak pantomime, I would have lost that case.

Still, now I had a crisis on my hands. Because sitting opposite me in my bedroom, sobbing uncontrollably, Crockett was saying, "Can you go and phone my mum? Tell them to come and get me."

I remembered reading about how to deal with a bad acid trip in a student survival manual. What was essential was reassurance. The pharmaceuticals amplified every wrinkle in the psycho-situation, and the means to pull things back was to fabricate a sense of safety, support and normality. At the expense of truth, if necessary. What they believed was happening to them, wasn't. And you had to make them believe that something else, something better, or more ordinary, was. Or would be soon. So I said, "Okay."

I went into the hall, lifted the handset and depressed the phone-hook. "Hello," I said. Pause. "Hello, yes, Mrs Campbell? Yes, it's Connor's friend, Roddy, from the band. Connor is here… No, no, no, he's fine, he's with me and…" so on. I paced out the dialogue. Crockett would overhear the concerned conversation and know that his mum now knew what was happening, would understand, and be on her way to collect him. We'd both sit waiting, talking. The mood would lift and as the effects wore off and he relaxed, we would crash out and wake the following morning, salvaged from the wreckage of the night.

I put the phone down, went back into my room and sat on the bed. Still sobbing but now with a hopeful-dog expression he hic-cupped, "Did you phone?" "Aye, I did. You heard me. They're on their way." He looked at me straight. And then, with a cold look and a hard edge to his voice, he said, "You *never* fucking phoned," and stood up and headed for the telephone.

I threw myself between him and the door. Took him by the shoulders, looked at him straight and said, "Crockett, it is after four o'clock in the morning and you are off your face on booze and drugs. Now, what are your folks going to say when you tell them that, or they figure it out? And what about me? Because one thing's for sure, it'll be my fault and you won't be coming back into Glasgow or going to gigs again any time soon. Goodbye to all that."

His expression changed as dramatically as if a prosthetic mask had been whipped off his face. He now wore a look of utter shock, collapsed back into his chair, put his face in his hands, leaned for-ward and said, "Oh fuck. Oh fuck oh fuck oh fuck." He looked up at me, his eyes wet and shining with gratitude. "Oh fuck man, I love you."

It brings to mind the rain-soaked monologue by the dying replicant in *Bladerunner*: "I have seen things you people would not believe... All those moments will be lost in time, like tears in rain."

But it was not time to die yet.

All that Glitters

I went through to Edinburgh pre-Christmas to see Gary Glitter. It was a tour called *Rocking the Recession* and – cue appalled disbelief – it was one of the greatest gigs I'd ever seen.

I could omit or deny it. Or re-tool the whole experience with testimony on how I felt uneasy, how a deeper instinct somehow cast a shadow. That there was something rotten in the state of Glam. And how, when the truth came out, that it justified my misgivings. "*Now* I know why I felt so uncomfortable."

Or that the truth corrupted it. Like I had eaten a sumptuous meal, only to be told afterwards that it had been poisoned.

But I'd be lying. This was just hilarious and glorious. All the hits, anthems each, compressed into this heaving little venue, perfectly judged between self-effacing send-up and utter seriousness; the decor, lights and Bacofoil costume like a Christmas roast. The cut-price, fallen-on-hard-times idol, the return to earning a crust offset against the glory days. The wave of love for him like a balmy tsunami.

It had a super-charged charm. It was such innocent fun. And it's in the memory bank, untouched and unsullied. The ultimate party.

A few months later, I arrived back from art school late one afternoon and the phone rang. It was Pete Irvine from Regular Music. Were we available that evening to support Gary Glitter at Tiffany's on Sauchiehall Street? We scrambled like Spitfire pilots and in a couple of hours were down there, sound-checking and soon after on stage in front of a generous but still arriving audience.

And the moral of the story is that it was an anti-climax. We didn't even get to meet Mr Glitter. We didn't even get paid. And, in its own little way, that sums up what it was like a lot of the time.

Maybe we didn't deserve to get paid. Maybe, like in *Barbarella*, the Matmos – the living energy source powered by evil thoughts – decreed that this was dirty money. That not being paid would be for our own good. That we would be poorer but sleep easier at night. And what price a clear conscience?

Who knows? But for all the subsequent monstrousness, I haven't lost a wink of sleep over it.

The Bubble

While all these things were going on in our world, outside there were other developments that occasionally drifted across our vision, like floaters.

One Monday morning, back of nine, all of First Year got on the bus that would take us to a study week at Culzean Castle on the Ayrshire coast. Driving down Renfield Street, there was already a huge queue round the Odeon Cinema for the 2pm showing that day of *Star Wars*.

Less significantly, Margaret Thatcher got elected, the Soviet Union invaded Afghanistan, the National Front and Rock Against Racism rose and fell, the World Cup happened in Argentina ("Football Yes. Torture No!" was the badge art students wore. Then Scotland tortured us). Coming soon, to a TV near you, the Falklands War.

Very early on the morning of the 9th of December, 1980, when my bedroom was a wreck with blankets and bodies after a gig the previous night, Temple burst in and said, "Jesus, have you heard? John Lennon's been shot dead in New York."

Not that we were self-absorbed. These wider issues do deserve mention, but they were not a distraction, far less a priority.

All Due Respect

We were fans of Tom Waits. Liked to think he embodied our post-Bohemian values. A latter-day, down-at-heel, low-life Sinatra defined by drink, dives, broads, late mornings, lonely nights. Either hunched at the bar or lurching around the naked city. *Heartattack And Vine*, with its sleazy, grinding, grunting riff, was one of our signature tunes.

So when Tom played at the Edinburgh Playhouse, we had to pay our respects.

Much of that day is lost. Most of it by the following morning. I met with Craig at lunchtime in the Griffin, who insisted that in homage to the great man we should drink Wild Turkey (American bourbon) on purpose. After which, we took the train through to Edinburgh. Peter came through to join us from Glasgow a bit later and we picked up where we left off. Killing time, sinking drinks.

Eventually, the time came and we slumped into our stall seats at the Playhouse and paid attention. It was, after all, why we were here. But it was very quiet. Tom on piano with only a drummer, semi-acoustic and a bull fiddle. More jazz than rock. It wasn't quite the same. The audience wasn't the same either. Older. A bit corduroy. We got sneery, sideways looks.

There was a break – or maybe not – anyway, we went to the bar where, above the gantry, was a black and white CCTV with a live feed to the stage. The reception made it look like he was playing inside a snow-globe.

But it was good enough. And we decided that it would be more respectful, "more Tom Waits", if we spent the rest of the concert there. Damn right, it's what *he* would do. We were true fans.

Kindred spirits. So we watched, or more accurately, ignored the rest of the concert from the bar.

It was a great night for the wrong reasons. After, I felt mortified that I had somehow contrived to feel proud about our conduct that night. But I was proud, at least, that I did feel ashamed.

A couple of years later, I landed a small part in the film *Local Hero* and was introduced to its star, Peter Riegert, who told me that he had once shared a flat with Tom Waits in New York. Wow. I was a handshake away from Tom Waits.

What I needed to ask him was, "Does he really drink as much as you read about?"

He said, "Naaah, he hasn't been drinking for quite a while now."

Deathwatch

The tremble of a thread in the knotted web said something was going on. There was a French film crew in Glasgow. And they were looking for extras.

Word was, you needed to turn up at the Glasgow Film Theatre one morning wearing unusual or offbeat clothes. There wasn't much more than the where-and-when basics. So I went along and shortly got enlisted, along with a horde of others. Soon, the specifics became clearer. Most importantly that it paid £20 a day. What an opportunity.

Despite the Gallic connection, the film was English language, called *Deathwatch* and starred Harvey Keitel and Romy Schneider. It was directed by Bertrand Tavernier and was an Orwellian sci-fi about surveillance that, it's said, foretold reality TV. It was set in a dystopian future, and what more dystopian a wasteland could there be than 1979 post-industrial Glasgow?

No spaceships or aliens this time. That would come later in 2011, when *World War Z* came to Glasgow and the city was the setting for a zombie invasion. And *Under the Skin* in 2013, when Scarlett Johansson as an alien kerb-crawled the city in a white Transit van, trapping, dissolving and consuming young men.

The following morning we assembled near Kelvingrove Art Gallery and got ready to board the buses that would take us, TARDIS-like, to this future.

Two figures compelled my attention. The first was a barn-door of a bloke. Larger than life. A gregarious greaser geezer character in a powder-blue suit and brothel creepers. He was definitely *someone* but he didn't have a name until later, when he became Robbie Coltrane. He had a proper acting part and, unsurprisingly, would be playing a "heavy".

The other seemed to be one and yet not one of the squad of professional extras who were now aboard the bus. He didn't get involved in the gossipy chatter about walk-ons in *Emmerdale*. He was older, perhaps in his forties, receding, dressed in a blue dog-tooth safari suit. Had an air about him, sitting on his own, taking up two seats, back against the window, a bit aloof. You could tell people were talking about him. But why? I eventually had to ask and was told that he was Sean Connery's brother.

Could this really be true? James Bond's brother was a £20-a-day extra like us? What did it say about sibling relationships and rivalries? What did it say about talent, opportunity and luck? About the razor's edge between success and oblivion? Could the universe really be so cruelly indifferent? It seemed so.

They had constructed a grim futuristic fairground somewhere near the Govan ferry. Fires in oil drums, reassembled junk and painted signs. It fitted in uncomfortably well against the backdrop of the city.

Few jobs are as boring and dream-crushing as being an extra. It's exacerbated by the allure and illusion of being in close proximity to glamour and success. Your role is to be peripheral, expendable and invisible. You're at your best if nobody notices you. If you could shout, "Behold, I am the greatest nobody and everyman," and be completely ignored, I'd say you'd nailed it.

Nothing was happening. We hung around. And hung around some more. Oh, and mooched about. There wasn't a camera in sight. The smoke drifted along.

Eventually a gilet with a clipboard came up to us and said, "Okay, you three guys are ze gang. You are ze tuff guys in zis place, *non*? Zis is your kingdom." And then we were told that Robbie the Heavy was going to chase someone around the wide perimeter of the fair. He'd barge through us, flinging us aside, surprising us, and we had to turn on him fiercely to retaliate and assert our authority – only to think better of it when we saw who it was.

By now it was a bit exciting. Something to do. A purpose. We were taking direction.

On the far side we could see activity and hear the shout "MOTEUR! ACKSHYON!" We followed the arc of this pounding, powder-blue rhino heading towards us. Until the inevitable collision. Bang. We scatter. Turn. Scowl and confront. Drop eyes and defer.

And that's how it went. On and on. Time and again. Robbie was not a natural athlete but seemed to come thundering towards us faster and more violently each time. Next time I would see him would be ten years later at Peter's wedding. As larger-than-life as ever. We never met.

The following day we were just making up the numbers. Somewhere far off I saw Romy Schneider and Harvey Keitel – big stars but very small – surrounded by personnel and boom mikes. They didn't appear to be doing anything. Again and again. Keitel's character in the film was called Roddy.

What you aspire to and can attain is all about proximity and distance. And the two are harder to identify and define than you might think. For me, not so much Gatsby – whose "dream must have seemed so close that he could hardly fail to grasp it" – but Father Ted instead: "*These* are SMALL. But the ones out there are FAR AWAY."

Eventually *Deathwatch* came out and I eagerly awaited our appearance. It lasted about three seconds. We can be picked out because I was all in white.

The Last Song

The last song I wrote for the band was called *Genius is Pain*. By now I was writing scripts for a character that Peter personified on stage: a furiously repressed, frustrated, resentful individual, permanently on the edge of breakdown. A bit like David Byrne in his outsize suit.

Genius is Pain

No one understands a single thing I ever say or do
No one knows about the kind of pain that I am going through
No one understands the kind of crap I have to tolerate
From imbeciles, idiots, incompetents, illiterates
No one realises and
No one sympathises
And I can't take it
And I can't fake it
Genius is pain
Genius is pain
Once again, for the record
Genius is pain

So don't talk to me about agony and ecstasy
Don't talk to me about the meaning of suffering
Don't talk to me talk to all the other fools you see
The brain-dead, boneheads, bloody ignoramuses
No one apologises
That's what I despise most
And I can't cure it
And I can't endure it

Genius is pain
Genius is pain
Once again, for the record
Genius is pain

Pain, misery and shame
Pain, misery and shame

So please go away, I want to be left alone
Please go away, can't you see I want to be alone
Please go away and please, please keep away
The dumb-bells, numbskulls, knuckleheads and chuckleheads
They're handing out the prizes
To the guys that I despise most
And I can't bear it
And I just won't wear it
But I'm nearly through, I'm nearly through
And this is now addressed to you
Genius is pain
Genius is pain
Once again and don't forget it
Genius is pain.

If we'd ever recorded it, I imagine it would have conjured the obligatory image of the narrator being dragged screaming out of the studio. Or maybe we could have ended it with a pause, followed by the disembodied voice of an analyst saying, "Okay, so that's our time for today. I shall see you next Tuesday, Mr…"

It was referred to in a *Sounds* feature about us from 1981, which referenced Lenny Bruce, Patti Smith, Elvis, Joy Division, H.P. Lovecraft, Bela Lugosi (in some depth, including how his ring was passed on to Christopher Lee), Basil Fawlty, John Lennon, National Lampoon, Antonioni, Jack Nicholson, The Cramps…

The lyrics seem to be all about dark nights and the possibility of making it home across the common ... There's a lot of huddling under blankets and listening to the rain beat against the windows ... The music is raucous roll, beyond punque ... Extremely funny or extremely serious is how they get on Genius is Pain ... 'Kill yourself laughing' might be a great title for [their] album.

Some word-cloud type sampling from another review: "hypnotically bizarre ... whips into a manic demonic thrash ... lurches violently, obsessively ... blitzed out version of rockabilly ... theatrical displays of mock gothic rantings ... irresistible rushes of twitching noise." The conclusion: "That the Dreamboys serve as a vehicle for Capaldi's immense talent is undeniable, yet their perverse treatment of the rock 'n' roll horrors is delightfully appealing. Don't take it all deadly seriously..."

The King of Gaelic Comedy

One night, Craig, Temple and I turned up for rehearsal and Peter
didn't. Nobody knew why. So we adjourned to the Griffin and
whiled away the night, imbibing and intermittently wondering
what might have happened to him.

Shortly before closing time he appeared. He'd had a hard day at
the BBC where he worked during holidays. Mostly graphics but
also as an assistant on productions.

A Gaelic comedy-sketch programme called *Tormod a Rithist!*
("Norman Again!") was being produced, which starred Tormod
MacIllEain (Norman Maclean). Outwith the Highlands and
Islands and the Gaelic World, Norman wasn't well known, but
within his own community he was a legend.

He was a cultural polymath, perhaps some kind of genius. An
accomplished Gaelic singer, he is still the only person to have
won both the Bardic Crown and the Piping prize at Gaeldom's
biggest festival, the Royal National Mòd (a.k.a. *ad nauseam*, the
Whisky Olympics). That was in 1967. And not only was he a brilliant impressionist and a natural comedian, he was a scholar of
the craft. He introduced Peter to stand-ups who were then far
from household names, like Richard Pryor and Steve Martin. He
recognised his talent and encouraged and nurtured it.

He also had a legendary, prodigious drink problem. God knows
what heights Norman might have hit had he not hit the bottle
with unerring accuracy at critical career junctures. Major opportunities, appearances, engagements, concerts and commitments
were sacrificed with shocking, ultimately predictable regularity.
Second chances, third, fourth chances came and went in an epic
parade of self-sabotage.

In late life, he was forced to quit, because every time he did hit the bottle it hit him back so hard that he ended up hospitalised. It was a choice between being alive or dead, take it or leave it.

That morning at the Beeb, it had gone well. A few things were in the can and the whole production crew were primed, ready to roll after lunch. But the main man did not reappear. It didn't matter that the production was on a deadline, that public money was draining like a burst water-main, that it might mean that this could be the last thing he would ever be asked to do for the BBC. It did not matter.

And so Peter was sent on a search and rescue mission to trawl the bars on and off Byres Road. Which he did, and because it was still early, on this occasion he managed to find him and bring him in. And the afternoon filming went on and that was it.

But lunchtime had been a mere aperitif, a soupçon. Now the main business of the day could begin.

That night, with a haunted, exhausted look, Peter related being dragged on a Homeric odyssey round Glasgow boozers, ending up in the Park Bar on Argyle Street. *Ceud Mìle Fàilte* (One Hundred Thousand Welcomes) is what it says above the door. If you have the *cianalas* (homesickness), you will find a cure there.

It's the home-from-home for Gaels in Glasgow and – of course – everybody there knew him, idolised him and – of course – wanted to buy him a drink.

Norman was hugely intelligent and had a sophisticated sense of humour. But that's not the humour that he took with him to the stage in the clubs, community halls and hotels of the Gaelic heartland. No, that was more music hall: part slapstick, part drag-act, part knockabout. And I think it always rankled with him; the feeling that he was always playing beneath himself. That he could never properly spread his comedy wings. That he was an eagle in a chicken coop.

And the longer the night in the Park went on, the more lofty, crabbit, scathing and scornful he became. In the end, Peter managed to get hold of his wife, who headed straight for the Park Bar. The torch had been passed and he signed off and took his leave.

The Forsyth Saga

As everybody now knows, the film director Bill Forsyth discovered Peter Capaldi singing in a punk band. He walked in on The Bastards from Hell and just *knew* that he had found his star. A truly amazing story. You might as well have my version.

One morning I was walking down Woodlands Road on the way to art school when I became aware of someone across the road. He had evidently clocked me and was now preparing to cross over to follow it up. In Glasgow, this was seldom good news so I upped my pace. Surely to God I wasn't going to have to make a run for it at this time of the day.

But there was something verging on the familiar about him, so I held off on the panic button when he caught up with me. He introduced himself and said he was directing an actress called Caroline Guthrie in a play. Would I be willing to talk to her so that she could attune herself to a Hebridean accent for the part? Having never met the guy, I was mystified as to how he could know where I came from, far less how I sounded. Maybe he was some kind of stalker. Sure, I said. I didn't think I had much of a Hebridean accent but if that was all… It was a bit of an unusual encounter and also a bit of a relief. A good day: I wasn't going to be assaulted after all.

I never got that phone call. But one night – Monday, the 26th of October, 1981; I have the ticket – we went to see what that other lovable Svengali, Malcolm Maclaren, was up to. His latest band, Bow Wow Wow, fronted by a half-Burmese teenage singer called Annabella Lwin, was playing at a club called Mayfair on Sauchiehall Street.

In the corridor off the main hall, I noticed Bill Forsyth talking to Peter. And talking and talking. And Peter listening and listening. For the entire gig. Bill didn't hire him for *Local Hero* there and then but he had certainly put him on notice. There was definitely something afoot.

That I subsequently got a small "Second Seaman" part in the film as a musician was about as likely as being hit by a meteorite. But I did.

The End: Not With a Bang

I can't remember where or when we decided to call it quits. We had to break up if we were to remain friends. But then we couldn't be the same friends anymore because we didn't have the common interest, the common denominator, the focus, the project. And we wouldn't see each other as much. We were headed down separate roads. I was heading overseas. Back to the Isle of Lewis.

The irony is that by then we had never been so in-demand and successful. And it had never been less enjoyable. The engagements we got were in big clubs and discos. Joanna's and Maestro's in Glasgow and Buster Browns and the Nite Club in Edinburgh. We did the John Peel Roadshow. Decent money too.

Our last gig was to be at Night Moves, a new top-floor club on Sauchiehall Street. It was a happening place for big bands. And because of the significance of the occasion, Billy Sloane, then a Radio Clyde DJ, was going to video it for posterity. It being a historic occasion.

All I know is that the gig *was* taped but without the sound. Which seems symbolic. Or some kind of metaphor. Maybe it still exists in Billy's vaults, alongside the master tape of our first demo, which he never returned to us. A silent movie with a gesticulating figure bellowing and screaming noiselessly, trapped in his own frenzy, like a bluebottle in a jam jar. If only we could hear him, we might know why he was so unhinged.

I can't even remember if it was a good gig. I think, by then, they had all blended into a kind of wallpaper. Nothing stood out about it other than that it was the last.

We wouldn't have to do this anymore, but that was more of a relief than a disappointment. We were free to go. Still, what *would* we do? We'd been on such a long corkscrew road together and, after finally hitting the motorway and heading for the city centre, the engine just gave out and we pulled over onto the hard shoulder, got out and started walking.

We were all going to be getting different buses into the future.

Part III

This Island Earth

Monday 4th March 1985, on my first day at work at An Lanntair.
Photo: Sam Maynard.

The Gun

After leaving art school and the band and Glasgow, I went home but kept returning to the city. I couldn't uproot just like that, I had to taper off. But each time I went back it had changed a little. The buildings were in the same place, with the odd addition or demolition, but pubs and shops would have new names, friends would have left or moved flat. I didn't have a locus, things kept shifting. There was a sense of being disembodied.

If there was a reason I was there this time, I don't recall, but I hadn't been gone all that long. A cousin of mine had a top-floor flat off Great Western Road that she shared with her boyfriend and a few others. There was also a flat-within-the-flat, through the broad hallway and up a steep stairway. A spare room, too, with a TV and a couch and it's where I stayed. This time. There was, however, an outside possibility that her younger sister might be coming for an overnight later on in the week. Might be a problem.

What I was doing in Glasgow was of no consequence. Still, it was good to touch base. Only it wasn't a base anymore.

One of the other flatmates was known to me. He was a Duncan, from Edinburgh, and if memory serves, his father was a senior legal something-or-other. I suppose he was at the university. Why not?

Small, wiry, animated, clever, unscrupulous and massively confident. That's how I would have described Dunk after a *Guardian* Blind Date. Maybe he grew up and went on to follow his father into the law, to dole out sentences and punishments to upstarts and reprobates like himself.

One Monday night a few of us were watching TV when we heard a startlingly loud bang. Loud enough for us to look at each other and say, "What *the frog* was that?" We turned down the telly and went to the window to look down into the narrow, dim, sodium-lit street. Nothing seemed to be amiss. Maybe it was a car backfiring, whatever that meant. And assuming cars still did that. We went back to the telly.

The rest of that week was rationed. Resources conserved to finance the weekend until, at last, the dog days dwindled and we arrived safely at Friday night. Here in His Nibs just off Sauchiehall Street, like so much wildlife round a watering hole, were other deserters and outcasts from the band scene. Among them Laurie, from the Cuban Heels, and ligger of legend Scott Macarthur. Drink begat drink. Rounds went round. The location changed. It became a kind of aimless drift along a meandering course through several pubs, ending at Night Moves in the small hours.

But, come closing time, we didn't want to stop. We went back to Laurie's in Kelvinbridge and drained cans of lager there, until there were none left and it really was over. I had to get back but I wasn't complaining because I was absolutely shelled. It had been one of those nights where you surf on a sea of booze, buoyed and carried along by the surge without somehow falling off. Now I was wiped out and being washed up on the shores of sleep. I really needed my bed.

Wearily, I climbed the tenement stairs. Scott was with me. I guess he was looking for a floor to crash on. When we got inside there was something going on in Dunk's room, which was first on the right. Some kind of party. Scott went in but I couldn't have been less interested. My sole ambition in life at that particular juncture was to get to bed. And I was on the threshold of achieving my goal.

I went up the internal stair and without even needing to put on the light, to my unutterable dismay, I saw there was someone asleep on my couch: the wee sister. It felt like walking at speed into a plate glass window. What could I do but go back down to join the party? They were bound to have a floor in there.

The Gun

The dog-eared, regurgitated memory of this affair flickers in my mind's eye like a broken black-and-white TV. On its grainy screen, Dunk is the ringmaster brandishing a curved ceremonial sword while his two accomplices are shouting at each other, role-playing and generally pissing about. There is a two-bar electric fire in the middle of the room. Scott has procured a can of lager and is drinking it in the corner.

God help me.

I didn't have to endure too much of it though. Fortunately, I was unable to cling on to consciousness much longer and sank into the deep void. I passed out on the carpet. At this race to destruction I was a DNF. Did not finish.

Now I was groping about sightlessly in some prehistoric Stygian cave. Crude paintings on the walls were barely discernible in the dim flickering light. Trying but unable to move away from the fire in the middle of the floor while a hostile tribe hammered at the door. Which is stupid. A cave doesn't have a door. How would that work? It just isn't credible. Until I began to come round to the idea that I was in fact awake. Or a version of awake. I was flat on my back on the floor. The room was in darkness and the only light was the orange glow from the two-bar electric fire a couple of feet away that was grilling the side of my face. Black body shapes were strewn about. And the hammering was inside my head. No. Inside the room. No. Outside. Getting louder. At the front door in the hall. Someone was desperate to get in.

Groggily and as urgently as I dared in my brittle state, I levered myself vertical, stepped over a body, went out of the room, and stood in front of the thumping door. As I turned the latch it swung in on me as if spring-loaded and I was pinned back by a large, heavily built, thick black moustache in a trench coat. There were two other looming silhouettes behind him and the moustache was shoving some kind of ID in front of my face. "Where's the gun?"

he barked. Good question. Where is the gun?

"Bewildered" doesn't even begin to cover it.

The three plainclothes barged in and flicked the switch; a violent white light flooded the room, blinding the human cockroaches in their nests. Too stupefied, drunk with sleep and disorientated to do more than blink and mumble. All were frisked and manhandled and the room filleted: mattresses and cushions lifted, drawers rifled. No weapon retrieved at that stage. Except the sword. The whole operation couldn't have taken more than thirty seconds.

Soon I sensed the cops adjusting. Coming down from the adrenaline rush. The edge softening. It wasn't a terrorist cell or a gangster hideout. It was just some stupid fucking students, as lethal and threatening as a Sunday school outing.

Dunk was identified quickly as the prime suspect and was now talking, explaining, applying a reasonable, modulated tone to his discourse. Setting the foundations for the narrative that would develop over the coming interrogation, which would perhaps ultimately flower in court. The sword was military memorabilia. He was a collector. An academic project he was doing. The more he wittered on, the more confident and assured he became, the more the police relaxed. They were fluent in Bullshit. Still, no shootouts today. They would be going home to their families.

All done, we were led downstairs, where two police vans were waiting with their engines running. Scott and I were shoved into the windowless back of one of them and at five o'clock in the morning, escorted from the tinned shadows to sit separately, forlornly, in Partick police station, bleached in fluorescent light. There was an Elvis poster on the office wall.

What had happened, it transpired, could be backdated to the previous Monday night. The big bang. Dunk and his chums had been horsing about. Perhaps he had a taste for the rougher side of life; bohemian, working-class, perhaps criminal, culture and its accoutrements. Maybe he was rebelling against his dad. And he did have a handgun. And like wee boys, knocking on the door and running away, he had fired it out of the window. The bullet had gone through the boot, back seat, front seat and engine of a parked Volvo. Doubtless, ballistics were involved but it was the testimony from witnesses that night, who had seen flashes from the window of the flat, that corroborated it. Only, they weren't gunshots. The chums had been running around with the lights out, taking photographs of each other by flash. Drama students for the night.

We were released a few hours later. I don't think they even bothered to take statements. We could have gone back home but we needed to process what had happened. Talk about it. We were still spooked. We needed a livener. The pubs opened at 11am.

Sitting in Tennents bar, I felt like I had just returned from outer space and was now in quarantine. To knackered and beyond. I was aware of the pull, the drag of gravity on my body. Scott had found his voice again and wouldn't shut up. He spoke the language of adrenaline and alcohol.

I have no idea if a prosecution ensued. If it did, I'd put money that Dunk got off with a ticking-off, a suspended sentence, or at worst a fine or a compensation payment to the car owner. Maybe his dad would have been involved behind the scenes. Who cares?

But, by now, the postponed weariness had come to reclaim me. The Benign Reaper. Accompanied by the bailiffs. I gave up and headed once more for home. Second time lucky. And finally, twelve hours later, at three o'clock on that Saturday afternoon, I climbed the internal stairs to the flat and lay down on the now vacant couch and closed my eyes.

The First Days of the Rest of My Life

After art school, I reverted to my default position: working on government job creation schemes (Manpower Services Commission). During the early years of the Thatcher administration, these were a means to keep the unemployment figures down. In Lewis, it meant mending unsurfaced peat-roads, village drainage schemes, fencing projects and so on: the kind of thing you do now if you're sentenced to community service.

Locally it was known as "job recreation". You didn't work if it was raining, which was more often than not. Or if the midges were bad, which was only frequently. We began just before the mid-morning tea-break that took us towards lunch, and we concluded mid-to-late afternoon when our foreman would fling his shovel into the van and say, "Chuck it, fuck it, we'll call it a day, boys."

One expert dole-monger, despite his best efforts, had been dragooned onto our squad. It was the only job he'd ever had in his life. Fortunately, it was temporary. He was granted asylum when a doctor decreed him medically unfit for work. This gave him an enhanced allowance and lots of free time to set his salmon net, smoke fags in the car, flog his catch – backdoor – to the hotels and get pissed on the proceeds.

It was a more generous, gentle, lenient time when being pathologically useless was officially recognised as a legitimate clinical condition that warranted state support. When his terminal ailment was diagnosed, his wife wiped her eye, bit her lip and said bravely, "I'm afraid poor Kenny will never work again."

With an Honours degree in Fine Art you were basically unemployable. Most managers would assess you as over-qualified or some kind of snob or snowflake or – perhaps more reasonably

138

– assume that you wouldn't fit in or get bored doing a "normal" job. A handful of graduates became art teachers, but most came to regard their time at art school as an over-extended gap year. The party now over, they returned home all grown up, got in line and retrained for a proper career. Joined the council.

I'd been the only person in my year to go to art school, so I felt like the last passenger pigeon. Lonely. Doomed.

In desperation, I applied for Voluntary Service Overseas (VSO), but they didn't want me either. No, not even in the Third World. I had a globally transferable anti-skillset.

Then a highly unusual job creation scheme came up in a new gallery called An Lanntair, which was opening in Stornoway. They were looking for a supervisor and a couple of part-time assistants. It was a bespoke opportunity, but by then I knew my place, my station in life, so I applied to be an assistant. Whereupon I was told that because I had just finished another job creation scheme, I was ineligible. I could only apply for the top post. It seemed as pointless as filling in a risk-assessment before going over the top at the Somme. A bitter blow, but what the hell, might as well.

Shortly after I applied, I got word that I would be interviewed. So, at least that was something. But wait. What's this? The evening before the interviews there was going to be an "informal social gathering" of all the applicants and the founding committee on the new premises. Oh dear God. Please. No. Was there nothing straightforward left in life?

It was exactly the charade that I expected. A kind of banal, mask-less masquerade. All the applicants eyeing up the oppo-sition. Drinks and snacks. Would I like wine? Ah, not on a weeknight – juice, please. Committee members mingled between us and chattered amiably and inconsequentially before chucking a grenade into the conversation: "So, what do you think of the premises?" And then it was on-point, stand-to-attention interview mode: "Well, yes. It has huge potential, it's a great site, etc."

After we had gone, the committee convened, presumably to discuss how we had performed. To dissect our social skills, decode our body language and comment on our clothes and haircuts. I went to the Mac's Imperial, my old stomping ground. Seldom had I been in such grave need of a pint.

My friend Robbie Neish, from Glasgow, had been the year ahead of me in art school and had designed the Lanntair logo. He was on the committee and when the meeting was over he appeared in Macs and told me that he had stood up for me. Said that the art director at the Scottish Arts Council had thought I was a bit of a loser because I hadn't really done anything since I'd left art school. Robbie had said that I'd been in a band and even been in *Local Hero*. I hadn't mentioned this in my application or during the schmooze. It somehow felt incongruous, inappropriate. A bit gross. Like showing off. It might give the wrong impression of the kind of person I really was.

The next morning we had builders in the house working on an extension. The Pongo, Johnny Kruger, Warhorse and the rest of the crew were having their tea-break in our ruined kitchen under the open rafters. They asked where I was going and when I told them about my interview, they said that I was wasting my time. That "an Englishman is going to get that job".

Well, an Englishman didn't. *I* did. And when I did, I clung to it like a barnacle to a rock.

Although it was technically still a job creation scheme with a guaranteed lifespan of only one year, it felt different. It was a real job. Something that I might actually be qualified to do or have an aptitude for. I was a boss! I had a telephone and, a few months later, got a typewriter. I designed posters and publicity, wrote reports and copy. I wondered if, in time, I might even become eligible to the opposite sex.

Onwards. We imported, produced and presented exhibitions and, in the evenings, promoted music events. It was important to develop an audience that would still be interested after the initial novelty wore off. To become relevant, indispensable. There was no real tradition of visual arts, no infrastructure, little overall public awareness and plenty scepticism. Everything had to be learned from scratch.

And the best way of learning anything, of course, is to make mistakes. Lots of them. The best kind of mistakes. Which is something I really was good at.

Odyssey

Most of the carriers we used at the gallery handled valuable works with the same care they would their usual cargo – say, a sack of potatoes, tractor tyres or an outboard motor. So we began to hire vans to collect and deliver exhibitions ourselves. Monthly, I would traipse up and down the A9.

This time, the paintings to be returned to their owners were all, frustratingly, a couple of inches too large for a standard Transit van. We needed a bigger vehicle, but there weren't many options. In fact, there was only one available and it was not from an established van hire company.

It was to be delivered on Thursday morning in time for us to load the exhibition and to catch the lunchtime ferry. Late morning a guy showed up in the office in his boiler suit and said it was parked round the corner. I asked if there was anything I needed to know. He said no. I gave him a cheque. Money upfront.

Then I went round to collect the van and bring it round to load up. But when I went to start it, I saw that the ignition was a spaghetti of wires, sprouting and spiralling out of a ragged orifice in the dashboard. Time was already short so I ran upstairs to phone about this. While listening to my anxiety ring out to nothing, the guy reappeared. I had forgotten to sign his cheque. Oh yeah, that's right, there was something he had forgotten to tell me. So he gave me a quick lesson on how to start the van by turning a screwdriver in the detached plastic disc at the end of the wire-ball.

Alarm bells? You could say, but I muffled them. There really wasn't time to make alternative arrangements. We hadn't had much choice in the first place. And you can travel a great distance on hope.

Odyssey

It was snowing as I drove onto the ferry and a bright frosty moonlit evening in Ullapool as I was towed off by a MacBrayne's lorry. Which got the van started. There were obviously some matters of concern but as I headed for Inverness and got a few miles under the belt, I began to un-tense, relax a little. Teething troubles, hitches and glitches. Just drive. I must have been about halfway when despite the white, almost-daylight moonlight on the illuminated snowfields, I began to notice the headlights getting dimmer. The engine wasn't charging the battery. And the indicators weren't working.

I thought if I could make it to Inverness where the streets were lit, I could hunker into a B&B and put together a strategy to sort all this out. But I stalled in the middle of one of the busiest roundabouts in the Highlands.

The hazard lights didn't work either and it took about fifteen minutes for the police to arrive. During which time I endured a cacophonous, howling symphony of car horns and shouted abuse. All the while having to work out a plausible explanation for the exploded ignition and the screwdriver trick when the cops did turn up. But I just couldn't think of one.

As it happened, it wasn't necessary. The cop hopped in and asked me to shove over. It seemed that coaxing and resurrecting life out of a dead battery was a matter of personal, perhaps professional, pride. And sure enough, with a sensitive, masterful, virtuoso combination of throttle and screwdriver, he mustered just enough kick to turn it over and start the engine. "There you go," he said. "The magic touch." His achievement eclipsing his duty. I'd guess it was the highlight of his day.

So I made it to a B&B in Inverness, after all. And when I got behind the wheel the next morning, the engine started first time. But choking clouds of black, rubberised smoke blew up over the windscreen. I shut it off and opened the bonnet. God knows

143

why, because whatever's under there is meaningless to me. Pipes and wires and stuff. But even I could spot a broken fan belt. If I'd had a wife or girlfriend, I could have asked for her nylons to bodge it – I'd heard that was a handy motorists' tip, back in the day. Instead, I had to make do with phoning a garage.

They put in a new fan belt and got on with a most basic health check. They had to call in an electrician. Half the fuses in the rack were replaced. They asked me where I was headed. "Edinburgh and then Glasgow." "In this? Good luck, mate," and shook their heads, doubtless marvelling at my pluck. Two hours I'd been in there and it was after lunch before I got going. Still, the worst was over. Or at least postponed.

Outside Inverness, for purely selfish reasons, I picked up a young, studenty woman who was thumbing her way to Edinburgh. It was for company, moral support and possibly a push, if need be. But when I had to turn off for a quick delivery at Kingussie, she took her kit and her chances and got out to stand by the side of the A9. I thought, "You'll go far. Perhaps further than me."

I reached the Scottish Arts Council's store in Edinburgh minutes before they closed for the weekend and dropped off the work that we had borrowed from their collection. Then I headed off on the M8 through to Glasgow.

It was on that leg I noticed that the needle on the dial indicating engine temperature was jammed in the red. Running out of ideas, I pulled over to a service station for a while to let it cool down, topped up the radiator and carried on. Seemed better. Didn't it? Of course it did. If I could make it to Glasgow, I could re-group...

The next morning, the mechanic at the garage in Partick said it was because there was no antifreeze. "Feel that," he said, fondling the bottom pipe from the radiator. "Totally cold. Shouldnae be like that." Well, it only cost me a tenner.

I spent the rest of that Saturday driving round Glasgow returning Peter Seddon pastels to private lenders. The engine temperature was fluctuating between normal and off-the-scale infra-red. Perhaps it would sort itself out when there was less stop-and-start.

By four o'clock it was dark and I was on my final task of the day: going to B&Q in Anniesland to collect a fibreglass side for a bath. Then on to Dundee to collect our next exhibition. Once I got on the dual carriageway the needle stopped fluctuating. It leaned hard up against the outer edge of the red zone. I had to stop. Had to. This couldn't go on. I pulled over at a service station and saw a dim light from a garage on the far side of the carriageway. It was pitch black and freezing hard again. It took me ten minutes or so to sprint over the twin-stream metal river without being flattened and I walked into the yard.

I suppose it's just as well it was cold, because it meant I was wearing my layers, a thick jersey and a heavy overcoat. So when the Alsatian guard-dog grabbed my arm it didn't actually break the skin. I wrenched free from the crazed animal slavering at the end of its chain. It wasn't a garage, after all. Naw, the guy could-nae help me.

"Never, never, never give up," said Churchill. It's on my fridge. I thought that if I could make it as far as Stirling, I could re-group… Freewheel as much as possible and let the engine cool down. A natural kind of air-cooling, especially in these temperatures. Like a vintage VW. I am nothing if not creative.

On I went until, on the outskirts of Dunblane, the engine just stopped and I freewheeled onto the hard shoulder. There wasn't a death rattle but it was hardly unannounced.

It could have been worse. I was close to the Dunblane Hydro hotel and I phoned the breakdown services from a payphone there. Then, for the second time on my journey, the police arrived on the scene. Then the recovery vehicle and a couple of interested passers-by, who became engaged bystanders. The diagnosis and recovery began. Supernaturally, with a turn of the screwdriver the engine started first time, but it now made a dismal, sick, hollow, donking sound. This was the death rattle. "Naw, son, that engine's fucked. This'll no be going anywhere anymair."

There was a train station in the centre of Dunblane within walking distance, so I abandoned the van to make my way to Dundee by alternative means. And as I walked along the hard shoulder at eight o'clock on that freezing Saturday night in mid-winter, buffeted by the pressure waves of heavy vehicles and buses, with a holdall and the side of a bath like a surfboard under my arm, I thought how fortunate I was not to have had any paintings left to deliver.

Sin

How fair is thy love, my sister, my spouse! how much better is thy love than wine! and the smell of thine ointments than all spices!

The Song of Solomon

IIt's said that the male libido is like being handcuffed to a madman. Or, less dramatically, like being dragged along by a boisterous spaniel on a leash. While at art school, some years after mislaying my virginity on the concrete steps behind the village telephone exchange on a black, rainy, sodium-smeared winter's night, I was granted the greatest gift a young man could aspire to: an adult relationship. To paraphrase Homer (Simpson): The cause of – and solution to – all my problems.

It began in a student halls of residence in Dundee. I'd just returned from an art school trip to Paris and I was going to overnight it with a girl called Rona. And although it was never mentioned in planning, it couldn't not happen. Could it? The thought of it made me swoon.

I had first gazed at her across a pint and a pub table a couple of years earlier. She had come through from Dundee to see her older sister. One of her regular visits. She was about eighteen, nineteen. Composed, self-possessed. Pale, flawless, luminous, lustrous. Cropped red hair. A crisp, plain white, cotton blouse buttoned up to the neck. No make-up. No earrings. Unadorned. Nothing to hide or disguise or enhance. No need. Imperiously unaware of herself, she just let who she was do all the work. Effortlessly airborne on the thermal of youth.

I had the growing sensation, not so much of being captivated, as trapped. And that I had to do something. Make something happen. I didn't know what, but I had to try.

Between then and this night I failed so many times that eventually I must have run out of mistakes. Trial and error. More error. Better errors. Less bad errors. Each time I made progress, I blundered, squandered it. I didn't have the manual for beginning, far less building and establishing a relationship. The whole thing preoccupied, obsessed and oppressed me. I could not find a way. And yet, somehow, here I was on the cusp of closure.

Early evening, I arrived off the train from Glasgow, bought a bottle of Le Piat D'Or and got a taxi. When I arrived, we didn't embrace or kiss. It didn't seem appropriate or natural. It would have been too forward. If anything, it was formal and polite. The mood slightly awkward with an undertone of apprehension. Dominated by a Great Unsaid. Thought and action seemed to be on parallel tracks that would never intersect in a shared destiny anytime soon.

The place was ringingly, resoundingly empty. On this balmy summer evening, there did not seem to be a single person in the entire building block. A payphone stationed at the end of the long, tiled corridor for all the calls to families and boyfriends. Although I was a vegetarian she made me chilli con carne. And I ate it. In fact, she could have served me a plate of gravel and I would have eaten it. And enjoyed it.

Afterwards, we went to her room. Narrow, clean and functional. Nothing on the walls. No celebrity or cringe-inducing "Love is..." posters. Not a single soft toy propped against a pillow. In a peculiar way it was like neutral territory. In love and war, a Green Zone. I was relieved that I wasn't disappointed.

There was a basic dressing table against the right-hand wall and, into the corner along the opposite wall, a single bed. At the head of the bed, to the right, a window overlooking a carpark.

I sat on a low chair below the window and began to unpack some things I had bought in Paris.Little gifts, witty knick-knacks from the Pompidou Centre. Gave her some Shalimar perfume in a little bottle. Expensive. Showed I had class. That I was sincere.

It was a monumental effort to appear casual, nonchalant or any version of normal. I suppressed what I wanted to happen because I didn't dare articulate it. Not even as a thought. Like something in the corner of your eye that will disappear if you look at it.

But the concentration on self-distraction was exhausting, unsustainable. Try and think about anything, except the thing you want most in the whole world.

The air had become thick. The conversation increasingly trivial and stilted, drifting towards meaninglessness. There was a membrane between us. A surface tension that separated the present from fulfilled potential. I didn't know what to do. I had to do something. Words couldn't bridge the space or broach the barrier between us. I couldn't bear it anymore. And as she dabbed some perfume on her neck I stood up and began to kiss her.

I couldn't tell if I was the agent of my own actions. Whether I had jumped or been pushed. Either way, forced. I couldn't have stopped any more than if I had thrown myself off a high building and then changed my mind. I hurtled towards a barely imaginable inevitable.

From the moment of contact, everything coalesced, liquefied, emulsified. The sensation was of submerging into another medium. Another state of being.

I had expected, assumed, perhaps even prepared for resistance and rejection. After all, things have to be earned. Fought for. Deserved. And surely I couldn't deserve this. Here, though, was consent. Confirmation. More than that, it was approval. She *wanted* me to continue. I felt incandescent. Risen.

Glued together we toppled onto the bed. Drowned in each other. When, abruptly, to my shock and inexpressible despair, she pulled away, firmly, decisively. And in a fluent, fluid, continuous movement kicked off her sandals, shrugged her dress and disappeared under the duvet. All that was visible was the sunset of her hair on the pillow. In those brief moments between the poles of despair and fulfilment it is entirely possible that I suffered some form of psychological, emotional whiplash.

In a floundering, desperate panic, I set about removing my burning clothes. I might as well have been wearing boxing gloves as I unbuttoned my shirt. Why was it taking so long? I had lost all physical coordination.

Under the duvet was a sensual overload of musk, skin and body heat. A flaring moment I wanted to last forever even as it was already over, evaporating into the ether, condensing into memory.

When I turned my head on the pillow to look at her, she stuck out her bottom lip in a cartoon, little-girl sulk and said, "Aww, is that all *I* get?" I said, "There's plenty more where that came from."

And there was. An urgent, relentless, tidal flood. A reign of bliss. A beginner's *Kama Sutra*. During a hypnotised, stupefied exploration, with a hint of impatience, perhaps exasperation, she gently but firmly guided my fingers to the right spot. It wasn't just gratifying, satisfying, satiating, it was educational. Higher Biology.

At last, at some lost hour deep into the night, I passed out.

And woke in the pale, frugal, curtain-filtered light of dawn, our limbs entwined in a sweaty Celtic knot. As I looked down on her, she smiled faintly, indulgently, maternally and stroked my cheek with the backs of her fingers; there-there, there-there. Her eyes did not open.

That afternoon, she walked me to the train. We barely spoke. Wrapped in our own personal conspiracy. There was a strange, more naked, shyness between us now. A self-conscious awareness. As if some protective layer had been stripped away. Was it a shared shame?

Or, had we expunged and incinerated all the dross and baggage of the past in the furnace of the previous night, and now stood in a new place with a clear path ahead? Maybe it was just serenity.

I took a photograph of her standing against a fence but she was too abashed to look straight at the camera. The picture never came out.

Alive and Dead

We met at a wedding and were together for a few months. I even met her parents. She was a senior health professional, clever, attractive and a good laugh. And to this day, I can't say conclusively what went wrong.

One Sunday night in Glasgow we went to see *Alive*, the film about the Argentine rugby team who survived a plane crash in the Andes by resorting to cannibalism. Before it, we went for a curry. And, over the pakora, somehow my latent discomfort with our relationship launched into language. It began as a nebulous expression of discomfort but precipitated into a cloudburst: I didn't want "us" to carry on. Did I mean it? I don't know. I suppose so, because I said it.

Sometimes I wonder if I am like a reptile. Inert, stone-like, for long periods, but with the ability to move with startling quickness when required.

We finished our meal and walked along to the cinema, in silence. And when it was over, got into a taxi, in silence. Until we got into her flat, where, with a piercing wail, she threw herself onto the sofa and dissolved in tears. Strangely, I felt helpless, disconnected. As if I was in attendance at a family bereavement. All I could do was commiserate.

The next morning, I left to catch an early flight. But, having left, I couldn't leave it at that. I felt guilty. I expected her to ring – demanding an explanation, if nothing else. But she didn't, so a few days later I rang her. To see if she was all right. She was legitimately furious and wanted to know what the exact fuck I was playing at, phoning her like that. And then she called back to say, "Okay, now I've got that off my chest maybe we can talk.

I'll phone you at the weekend."

That Sunday evening, she talked wistfully about her day. She'd been through in Edinburgh with her friend Paula. A travel agent. They did this and did that. And when they got back to the flat, they found that Paula's hamster was dead. And because neither of them could bear to touch it, they threw the whole cage, wheel, feeding tray, toys, deceased rodent and all, into the bin.

I knew then, unconditionally, that it was over.

Divine Intervention

We were on a bus from London to Glasgow. Had been there for a few days at a concert, visiting galleries, eating out. A pause, a hiatus, the road ahead. Sun slatted through the rooflights. The green ribbon of landscape unspooled; punctuated and defined by buildings and construction. She slept for a while but now we were both awake.

To pass the time we each in turn answered questions in one of those celebrity personality quizzes in a Saturday supplement. When were you happiest? What is your most treasured possession? What is your guilty pleasure? What is your greatest fear?

I said my greatest fear was losing my mind. She said hers was not getting to Heaven.

This harmless, innocuous, casual answer had a curious, powerful resonance. A barely discernible yet terrible signal. A pulse from a distant star. It foretold consequences, decided a long time ago. And yet to come.

I believed in heaven – on Earth – but it wasn't the Heaven she meant.

In a phone call a couple of weeks later, she mentioned people I didn't know and some I did. Members of a fellowship. A Bible group.

When I next saw her, she sat me down and said she had something to tell me. "I've become a Christian." Well. So was I. Whether I liked it or not. Baptised in the Free Church of Scotland. But I knew what she meant. This was serious. It carried the same body-slamming impact as "I've met someone." Or "It's not you, it's me."

She had a new boyfriend. His name was Jesus.

From that point on, she would not come into a bar with me, would not come to the cinema, would not come to a concert. The framework of our relationship began to deconstruct. The foundation undermined, earth-quaked. Overnight, we no longer had the same interests, overlap of friends, or wanted to go to the same places. All we had was our shared history.

Could love survive adrift of its moorings? Or was that a definition of true love in its purest state? An independent, self-sustaining, abstract entity. Spiritual. Eternal.

One Sunday morning, I phoned her. It rang out. Nor was there any reply all that day until she finally answered at the back of nine o'clock. She had been to church that morning. Followed by an all-afternoon fellowship, followed by the evening service and a further fellowship… She had wanted to stay in church for the whole day. She didn't want to leave.

Her love for me now, such as it was, included all humanity. A great part of it was in the form of an elevated forgiveness. For my sins, inadequacies and imperfections, attitude, inability or refusal to understand or comprehend. She forgave me everything. A blessing from the highest moral ground.

Only I didn't want or need forgiveness, or understanding, or the balm of soothing words. I wanted things to be the way they were. What was wrong with that?

Over two long counselling sessions I purged myself to a Free Church minister. A known intellectual, who had endured his own crisis of faith. An honest broker. Someone who would sunder the impasse. See my side. Take my side.

He described what had happened in terms of revelation. She had discovered a talent or aptitude within herself, as you might find a hidden, unrealised gift for music or poetry. And she should be not just allowed but encouraged to express and develop it. To let it flower. To rejoice and glory in grace. She was among the most fortunate. And so was I to have such a person in my life.

But I did not feel fortunate. At all. It might have been an interesting point of view but it was not the answer I wanted. It was not impartial. I could not let it go. I fulminated about my frustration, irritation, confusion, and asked in a roundabout way about the ethics of carnal sin, which for me was now merely an arcane theory. He quoted the King James Bible: "But if they cannot contain, let them marry: for it is better to marry than to burn." (Corinthians 7:9)

As if it was a straight and obvious choice. I was not enamoured by either option.

So I re-engaged with her. Tried to reconcile our positions. Argued, persuaded, cajoled. Marshalled my skill and will, to win the debate. The argument. To win her round. I had to win.

But everything had become binary, reversed, polarised, absolute. The rules had changed. Black had become white, only there was no way to prove it anymore. The Earth is round but it just got flatter. Perhaps I was the one who wasn't living in the real world. Perhaps I needed to grow up. Put away childish things.

Reason would surely prevail, but the undertow of rage I felt at being cast in this farce made it difficult for me to be reasonable. I was either relentlessly prosecuting her with logic and evidence, which she parried and deflected with an iron serenity, or, exhausted, we were skirting hand-in-hand round a yawning, empty arena into which neither of us could step unarmed, or leave unharmed.

The lowest common denominator was one.

One time over a cold coffee, I evangelised to her on the theory of evolution. The genius, compelling clarity and irrefutable logic of it. She listened attentively in silence as my words took wing. And when, with a flourish, I finished my elegant summation she looked at me with what can only be described as unconditional pity, slowly shook her head and said, "And you actually believe that."

The official line is that "there will be more joy in heaven over one sinner who repents than over ninety-nine righteous persons who need no repentance." (Luke 17:7)

But I was not ready to repent. Not yet. I didn't qualify. I was among the righteous. Righteously angry.

Wiser, more temperate councils advised that the initial fervour would abate. The fever would break. Things would normalise. You'll see. Hold your ground. But I just couldn't do it. I could not suspend disbelief. I could not pretend. I could not believe.

The end was perfunctory. A routine ceremony that we had to go through. The last rites. With our joint agreement, the life support was switched off as we sat silently and solemnly by our own bedside. Remarkable only in that it felt so unremarkable. No wailing or gnashing of teeth. Just splintered sentences. Assembled silences.

Beyond the crumbled arguments we had finally agreed on something.

I can't remember if I even said goodbye or see you later. I don't think so. The relief was intoxicating. Overwhelming. I felt overjoyed. In the car, I punched the air. I was free. There was no prospect anymore of a destiny in shackles further down the road. I had escaped the prison of that future. The Gaelic word for love is *gaol*.

Next morning, I woke with a mental blackout and a knot in my stomach. Inexplicably, I felt bereft, nauseous, wretched, but could not immediately recall or understand why. And then I remembered. But the realisation did not convert my abject melancholy into joy. I did not revert to the exhilaration that I felt the previous evening as I drove home.

I felt as if I had fallen down a deep hole inside myself. From which there was no escape and where no one would ever find me.

Over the coming weeks, I could barely function. I had all the energy of a sack of wet cement. I began to feel myself coming apart. A zombie, crumbling as I plodded on. Each day, an obstacle course littered with insurmountable trivialities. Each night, sleepless. I drank like a cliché, to fill the hollowness. But it was never enough.

Was this what I had really wanted? Deep down? Did I engineer it? Was this what I deserved? Evidently.

As if to deepen my darkest hour and salt my misery, I was invited to participate in a Gaelic documentary that was being filmed on the West Side of Lewis. They wanted to use an authentic checkmating sequence on a chessboard as a metaphor for an ingenious political manoeuvre and wanted my help. They were going to use a set of Lewis Chessmen. That day, all day, hour after merciless hour, I hung around a large bungalow with a TV crew, waiting for my little set-piece as the rain curtained the moorland outside in grey. Inside, my soul squelched in my boots. The chessboard analogy now seemed wholly personal and specific. I might as well have been that self-same, lugubrious, walrus-ivory King, inexorably driven to his fate in a "mating net".

It. Was. Over. I had lost. Conclusively. The "argument", the relationship, the whole caboodle. OVER. If only I could admit it. I endured and endured until, eventually, I cracked.

I wrote her a letter.

It wasn't an on-my-knees, please-take-me-back effort. I knew that would be premature and counterproductive. The bombed city would need to be rebuilt brick by brick. No, this was a first step, intended to re-open communication channels. To suggest or infer that perhaps we, meaning I, had been hasty, that the circumstances had been unusually difficult and that on more mature reflection, having taken some time, we could still work things out. The subtext was that it had been a test and, despite it all, we had survived. That we would be stronger as a result. It was subtly drafted to make her reflect and reconsider. As well as, of course, to showcase my complex and benevolent humanity. Make her realise and appreciate what she had got – now that it was gone. But only temporarily. It could be reclaimed.

Nothing happened. Until a few weeks later, when I returned from work one evening and saw the blue envelope with the looping, sloped, familiar handwriting waiting for me inside the door. I opened it with frantic, tremulous excitement and anticipation. My fingers trembling, my heart hammering against my ribcage like a trapped animal, the possibilities already unfolding like a gorgeous kaleidoscope. It almost seemed as if I might need a welding mask to read it. At last, I had begun to believe in miracles.

She wrote only to say that she had found my letter "quite interesting".

One morning, years later, in another flat, in another city, with another girlfriend, I waited for my taxi to the airport. As it arrived the Bacharach and David song *You'll Never Get to Heaven (If You Break My Heart)* came on the radio. And I felt a lump rise in my throat.

Deep

I was always good in the water. I learned to swim in the sea and just kept going. And I had fancied diving since first seeing *The Undersea World of Jacques Cousteau*. Throughout school my ambition was to become a marine biologist, until my mother returned from a careers convention and told me that, apparently, you needed Higher Maths to do it at university. That night my chosen future was torpedoed and plunged to the ocean floor.

In the 1990s, the Lewis Sub Aqua Club was reformed. There had been a version of it in the Seventies, but it too had gone under. It was a different age. The age of wetsuits. Drysuits hadn't been invented or were not readily available. Wetsuits are adequate for warm-water diving, swimming and surfing. But at depth the bubbles in the neoprene are compressed, so it loses insulation. And after surfacing from a dive in winter, blue with cold, sitting in the front of a rigid inflatable boat (RIB) hammering at speed over the hard, corrugated sea, the wind chill will suck every last vestige of heat from your body until you are as stiff and cold as a day-old corpse. Old hands who had re-joined the club remembered these days. Proudly, if not fondly. Everybody seemed to have had a version of that *rigor mortis*-in-life experience.

After the long cooling-off period of the Hebridean winter, the sea is at its coldest in April and May. One such time, diving off the Isle of Scarp I had to wear full thermal underwear, long-johns and a sweatshirt, under my suit. And gloves. I had so many clothes on that the air trapped in my suit made it impossible to get under. Aggressive buoyancy. Even while flailing and porpoising on the surface, I could still feel the cold.

We began training in the swimming pool and learned the

basics, graduating to shallow boat-dives. Throughout, safety was the absolute priority. There was a far from exhaustive list of things that could go wrong and an anecdote for each one. And it seemed that with each incident reported through the diving network, the list got longer. It was probably an advantage if you didn't have much of an imagination.

The first commandment was that you never dived alone. You were paired in the buddy system, and you looked out for and after each other. You were respectful of the weather and tides. On a dive, you communicated with a few basic hand signals: thumbs up for going up, down for down; an "O" with your thumb and index finger for "okay"; wobble your hand if something isn't right. If your buddy indicated "up", you went up. No questions, even if you'd discovered a chest with the Missing Treasure of the Incas on the seabed.

You didn't dive with a cold and especially not with a drink in you, even from the night before. The mantra was dive within your limits, within the parameters of your experience.

Most importantly, as a club, as a group, you needed to be organised. When you got to a dive site you not only needed a buddy, you needed someone up-top to pick you up at the end of the dive. So there would usually be four in the boat at the outset. Typically, a two-up, two-down system.

Boat diving is safer than a shore dive because you can be retrieved if you have drifted. The boat will come to you. On a shore-dive you have to find your own way back. You might have lost your bearings or miscalculated the distance or the air you have left in your tank.

There are various classifications of Advanced (or Adventure) Diving: drift-diving, wreck-diving, night-diving, deep-diving. As I progressed, I had done it all but deep-diving, which is classified as below thirty metres.

Cave-diving? Not classified. That's for nutters.

Each of these disciplines comes with specific hazards and chal-
lenges – mainly, getting lost or trapped – but deep-diving has a
narcotic dimension. In older, more romantic times, the hallucino-
genic effect of nitrogen narcosis was called "the raptures of the
deep". Nowadays, it's just plain "narked". We've lost the poetry.
If you think of diving as the polar negative of mountaineering, I
suppose it's the equivalent of going into thin air. Extremes.

Once upon a dive, one of our most experienced colleagues,
Gordon, had unwittingly, carelessly, gone past his planned depth.
He began to notice that his dive-watch was behaving weirdly. It
was going backwards. Anticlockwise. But being technically very
savvy he was able to work out what had happened. A cog had
become displaced in the gearing mechanism. With a little more
thought and application he even figured out how to fix it. Not
necessary. As he began to surface, he was intrigued to see that the
watch fixed itself.

You had to build up to it. If, for example, you had never tasted
alcohol and one day necked a half-bottle of whisky, chances are
you would be much the worse for the experience. So there was an
element of building up a tolerance for deep-diving. A biological
familiarisation process. Bit by bit, depth by depth.

The usual drill was to meet on Wednesday night and plan
the weekend dive. Where, when, who (was going to fill tanks),
whose RIB? Soon you came to realise that these precise coordinates, instructions, personnel and equipment specifications were
more like suggestions or estimates. If we met at the clubhouse
at 8am, it was likely to be after nine before everyone showed up
and anything up to 10am before we got away. That all-important
organisation and commitment was sometimes lacking.

One gorgeous summer Sunday, as had been agreed, I arrived
at the clubhouse at 7am, and sat in my car for over an hour. As

per the drill, I had spent an abstemious Saturday night by myself at home.

Nobody turned up. I went back home. I can't remember if I went back to bed.

I began to classify those occasions when we *did* get a dive as special. Rare. Increasingly so. Opportunities to be seized with alacrity. Who knew when the next one would come along?

Around this time Gaelic television was taking off and the drama series *Machair* was being filmed on the island throughout the summer. The series was now finishing and there was to be a wrap party on a Saturday night at RAF Stornoway. So that was the weekend taken care of. Something to look forward to.

And as expected it was a good night. More than that, a heavy night and a late night. A taxi dropped me off sometime after 2am. It's all a bit vague.

The next thing I knew was that my alarm was ringing. Which was confusing because I didn't have an alarm clock beside the bed. It was the phone in the stairwell. I forced my way through the pain that had been foisted upon me prematurely, and went to the phone. There was no hello, just: "Fancy a dive?" What could I say? I couldn't afford to pass up this scant opportunity. Could I? Of course I could. Not today, not today. So I said, "Uh... yeah, okay?"

"Cool. Can you be at the clubhouse in half an hour?" At which point I must have had a moment of clarity because I said, "No. Give me an hour."

It was never going to happen I thought as I took three aspirin and stuffed my kit into my holdall. We'll be waiting for bloody ages for whoever else is coming, then we'll spend hours fucking about and eventually, by the time we do go over the side, if that ever happens, I'll have recovered enough.

Dutifully, I arrived at the clubhouse. Within the hour. Waiting there was Allan and two other senior club divers. There was a 4x4 and a RIB was on the trailer. I slung my bag in the back of the car and got in the passenger side. "We're doing Braga Rock," and we screeched off.

Braga Rock is a long reef off Skigersta in Ness in the far north of the island. Most of it is below the tideline. It's about an hour's drive from Stornoway and we were there in forty-five minutes. As we skimmed out through the huge green swell, it occurred to me that less than a couple of hours earlier I had been asleep and about to wake up to a substantial hangover. I would have welcomed a minor postponement.

The outboard slowed and began to idle and as we heaved up and down on the mountainous swell, Allan looked at me and said, "Ready?" I said, "Yeah." And with that we adjusted our facemasks, put our regulators in our mouths and rolled backwards over the side.

The sea today was a swirling, pea-soupy green murk. Active water. Visibility was limited. Down we went through it. Down, down. More down. Most of my diving had been in the fifteen–twenty-five metres depth range. It's actually where most of the action is in terms of sea-life, and I had a basic calibration in my head as to depth relative to surface. But this was confusing. Most likely because of my medical condition. We kept sinking but I couldn't yet see the sea floor.

Then far below it began to emerge. Some kind of blurry but definite plain. And as we bottomed out of our descent, I looked at my depth-timer. It said 37.5 metres. That's over 120 feet deep, in old money. Or twenty fathoms, if you prefer. I now had the full set of Adventure Diving badges. Even more adventurously, I was doing it while brutally incapacitated with a hangover.

At depth you need more air in your suit to achieve neutral buoyancy. I didn't know that. My inflation button didn't seem to be working. While I struggled with it, Allan had dug out a huge crab from the sandy bottom. We were hovering over some kind of crater and at that moment I knew with absolute certainty that I was never going to see the surface or breathe the air of earth again. That I was going to die down there. The perimeter of the crater represented the ragged edge of terror. Everything I had ever been most afraid of was trivialised by the enormity of this present, mortal dread. My mind had become a vacuum, a huge bottomless void. A consciousness black hole. Linear thought was pointless. It would vanish in the negative space. There were no coordinates and there was no direction because there was nowhere to go. It was hopeless. It was the end.

The flooded brightness, even at that depth, was punctuated with sudden periods of dark shadow as the clouds hurried across the face of the sun. Like a slowed-down strobe. Each time it happened I couldn't tell whether I was losing consciousness, blacking out, or whether the external world was disappearing around me, eclipsing, dissolving into night in the middle of the day.

I became aware that Allan was staring at me. He gave me the okay sign as a question. I wobbled my palm and he jerked his thumb up. Again I pushed some air into my suit. Again nothing happened. Allan came over to me and held down the inflation button hard on my chest until enough air went in and I started to move up.

Because of the length of time at depth we needed a decompression stop and, at six metres or so, inflated a tall fluorescent surface marker buoy on a cord to show our position. Pendulum-like, we hung suspended at the end of this long filament with Jacob's Ladders of sunlight streaming down through the green water, framing, scaffolding us. Allan began to gesture, offering me the crab, evidently asking if I wanted it. I fleetingly wondered if he was entirely sane. He let it go and it dropped in slow motion, half stone, half giant spider, groping and scrabbling against nothing into nothingness.

After hanging off the ocean's cliff face for what seemed an age, we headed for the surface once more. Bursting into the atmosphere, feeling the wind and looking around, I could scarcely believe how far we had drifted. Braga Rock was in the distance, to the north, crowned with spray. When we had gone over the side, it had been south of us. There was no sign of the RIB and we were alternately hoisted skywards and plunged into a liquid trough with each deep breath of the open ocean.

Not this now. Not lost at sea. A helicopter rescue. The Scottish news reporting that hopes are fading for two missing divers lost in the Minch… search teams continue to scour a wide area…

And then, a glimpse of orange. A toy RIB in the distance. The others had been following a search pattern and we were recovered. As I got hauled up over the side I estimated that it was probably about the same time that I would have been getting out of bed at home in real time, had I not answered the phone. Or just said no.

It was the first dive of the day. Later that afternoon, following the appropriate dive interval, there was time for a less adventurous, shallower exploration-dive closer to the coastline. It was the very last thing on earth that I wanted to do but I knew I had to get back on the (sea) horse or there was every chance that I would never ever dive again. So that's what I did.

Re: Cycling

I got on my bike because of coffee. In the office I found that by the end of a day depleting the filter jugs from the café next door, I was so wired I was self-generating static electricity. Polyester curtains would lift when I went past, supermarket plastic bags clung to my legs, my hair would crackle. Something had to give. I could ease up on my intake or...

My brother wanted to borrow my car for a month, so I began to take my bike to work. Seven miles there and seven back each day. Then extended commutes. Then long weekend runs. Touring holidays. Unburdened by relationships, family commitments, financial pressures. Happy days, if only I'd known it.

I remembered the cyclist in Skye who had floated past us over twenty years earlier, as we buckled under our rucksacks packed with rocks. It had taken me that long to catch up with him.

The hardest thing about being a certified cyclist in Lewis was the exposure. Not the relentless wind, rain, hail and cold, in all its degrees, variations and combinations. No, it was that I was tuned in like a police radio-receiver to an imagined narrative emanating from each and every car that commuted past: "That's what's-his-face, isn't it? What's going on? Why's he on a bike? It makes no sense. Where's his car? It's pathetic. You'd think he could afford one with the job he's got. Good money for doing fuck-all. I think he lost his licence. I heard the police stopped him the other night. Why didn't he just leave the car and take a taxi? They not teach you that at university?"

It took me a long time to shut that down and learn not to give a flying squirrel monkey's toss about this imaginary snark bouncing off the inside of my skull like a radioactive tennis ball from a primitive computer game.

My Uncle Calum Iain didn't spare me. I didn't need to imagine what he thought. Because he told me. "Passed you on the bike the other day," he would cackle, shaking his head. "Jesus H. Christ. Your face was that red I thought it was going to burst. You're not fit. That's a young man's game. You're too old for that."

But as the months and the miles went by I found that sweet spot, a healthy routine. The hot pumping blood flow on a long ride rinsed and irrigated my brain. The flush of sweat, the metronomic stomp on the pedals was a kind of self-inflicted pummelling massage. The immediate task in hand displaced the dead weight of other problems.

Not that the medical profession concurred. By the time I was called up for a routine health check I had thousands of cycling miles on the clock, didn't smoke, drank only at weekends, was a pescatarian and had a relatively stress-free life. Alarmingly, I was told that my blood cholesterol level was "raised". I was given a skip-full of leaflets and pamphlets that told me what to eat and do. Everything I was already doing. My brother Iain got the same prognosis, while Tormoid, a fellow weaver, was congratulated on his admirably low levels and told to keep up the good work and continue his exemplary diet and lifestyle. Which, according to him, began each morning with a large fry-up and ended at teatime with a meaty feast. Followed by pudding.

Teth is Tioram: Hot and Dry

It was the summer that Miguel Induráin won his fifth consecutive Tour de France. And we were in France, with an exhibition that was part of the Festival Interceltique de Lorient in Brittany. I was to set the show up ahead of schedule, then Iain would come out and join me and we would take our bikes on our own personal tour de France before returning to Lorient after the festival had commenced.

That first morning at breakfast in the hotel, I couldn't stop rubbing a raised, hard, red area on my arm. About the size of a five pence piece. It was infuriatingly itchy. A mosquito bite, according to my host. Back in my room, I scanned the ceiling and, sure enough, there were two of them. Barely visible against the white plaster. Such slight, delicate things. I rolled up my copy of *Cycle Sport* magazine, stood on the bed, whacked the first one and was taken aback at the fat, dark-red, two-inch smear of blood it left on the ceiling. My blood. The other one had been less greedy. Maybe an inch.

The exhibition opened a few days later and we prepared to take off. No real plan, just head south, Nantes, the Loire, the Camargue, head for La Rochelle and Île de Ré, after that wing it. We had our map.

The one thing cycling in Lewis does not prepare you for is *le chaleur*. The heat. The sun beat down on us balefully, indifferently, as we toiled on drenched in sweat. Salt caked round the rim of our lips as minerals leached from our bodies. Every town, we needed a pit-stop for fluids, refilling water bottles. As we progressed it seemed that we visited the same café over and over again. Except for the one where I walked briskly through the door and a sleeping dog I'd tripped over leapt up and savagely clamped his jaws round my calf.

When I mentioned this back in the UK, the first question I got asked was, "And did you get a rabies shot?" I did not.

There were intermittent periods of joy, such as when we cycled on a narrow traffic-free road through the cool, dappled greenery of a small wood until emerging into the sun again, the dial set at permanent noon.

Campsites were plentiful. Every town had one on its outskirts and as the sun began to lower slowly over another baking, suffocating, airless afternoon we decided to call it quits. We set up the tent, dropped the panniers and cruised into town for some supplies.

Later that evening, in these most unseasonable conditions, we crawled into our Vango Force 10 mountain tent. Although getting dark, it was still stifling so we just lay on top of our sleeping bags in our underpants and passed out. We'd earned it.

Next morning, not immediately but soon, I became increasingly aware of the mosquito bites I had acquired through the night. I subsequently counted between seventy and eighty. My brother had none. Over the next day or so, these matured into constellations of hard hemispheres pushing up under my skin, each crowned with a weeping, crusty red nipple.

The following afternoon, freewheeling downhill at speed through an unmarked crossroads in a featureless fieldscape, I was T-boned by a car and sent skidding about twenty feet across the tarmac into a dry ditch. I must have left a square yard of skin on the road. It was over before I realised it had happened. Too quick even for the pain, which now body-slammed me after-the-fact. All I could do was try to breathe. But I couldn't. But I couldn't not. From this point on breathing and staying alive had a price: agonising pain. Till then, I'd rather taken it for granted.

The driver made all the right reassuring, apologetic noises. It didn't appear that there was anything broken. He poured some mineral water over my raw flesh. No harm done, and left. My front wheel was buckled and the front brakes had to be loosened off in order to continue. I couldn't go on. I could. I couldn't. I'll go on. What else could I do?

We made it to the next identikit village, stopped at the pharmacy for painkillers and iodine for the road rash and booked into a tiny hotel. The next morning I woke simultaneously sweating and frozen in agony. I knew I had to move but could barely bear to do it. I needed a doctor.

He was from Mauritius. Interesting. We talked a bit about that and – incidentally – the scope of my injuries. He declared that I had broken some ribs but that I would need an X-ray to confirm. We were driven to a hospital in some kind of medical vehicle. I had to hand over my credit card before going in. Prone in the radiology theatre, the doctor and nurses looked at each other and marvelled at my skinscape of mosquito bites, which now resembled a satellite image of the surface of Mars.

Incredibly, the X-rays revealed that my ribs were not broken, just severely bruised. So there was no medication, no bandaging, just a bill. Three days later, we were able to leave the hotel and made it to Cognac, where we got the wheel fixed. And managed a visit to the Hennessey distillery. And then we headed back north.

Each day was the same. Crippling, debilitating, gasping pain in the morning and a slow barely perceptible amelioration throughout the day on the bike. Eight hours later it was always better. Lying down was hell. A bed of nails would have been as comfortable but I couldn't sleep standing up. That would have to wait until parenthood. I wasn't a yogi.

A year later, if I pressed two fingers against a precise point on my ribcage, it still hurt. And in time, I began to notice a hard lump on my rib. I went to the doctor and got X-rayed. Nothing showed up. Nothing to see here.

It could only have been a fist of gristle that had formed round the stress point on the bone as some kind of natural bandage. In time it disappeared. And then a condensed lump of fat – a lipoma – raised itself on the same latitude on my back. Until I finally got that removed so my shirts would fit properly.

I thought of it as a tremor, a shock-ripple through my body that had finally been released, fifteen years later, having travelled through bone, flesh and ultimately skin until its energy had been absorbed, assimilated and dissipated. The lipoma in the surgical dish was the geological remainder and reminder of a past meteor impact.

Fuar is Fliuch: Cold and Wet

I was due some days off before the end of the financial year. I was also due to take part in an adventure race called the Western Isles Challenge in May. This was a team event involving cycling, running, canoeing and orienteering over three days through the Outer Hebrides archipelago, from the Isle of Barra to the Butt of Lewis. I was the designated cyclist for our team, The Demon Barbers.

So I decided I would get some training in and do a cycle tour of the north of Scotland. From Ullapool, up the north-west coast, along the top towards Wick and Thurso, and back. Assynt in Sutherland was visible across the Minch from out my back door (on a good day), but I had never been north of Ullapool. It's because the mainland meant Glasgow, Edinburgh and Aberdeen, which were all via Inverness. Why would you go to Kinlochbervie? Other than to land fish and crustaceans.

At six o'clock on Monday morning, in the dark, with a head-lamp, I cycled into Stornoway to catch the early ferry. I was going to keep this simple: travel light. No tents and sleeping bags and that malarkey. I would call in at the tourist office in Ullapool straight off the boat and book some B&Bs in advance. Maybe the odd hotel. I really didn't need the discomfort of cold-weather camping and the hassle of finding sites and figuring out food. This was training but also a holiday, albeit a bit out-of-season.

That mid-March morning, when I arrived outside the tourist office I was stumped to find it shut. In fact, it had been shut for six months: "the season" had ended the previous September. Sellotaped on the inside of the glass door was a page torn from a notebook, on which was written in faded biro a handful of B&B

phone numbers that might be operational at that time of year.

I couldn't be arsed taking the names. Anyway, I didn't have a pen and paper. I would just have to plan my stop-offs for the main centres where I could be confident there were people, places, accommodation. First of these, the Culag Hotel in Lochinver.

It was only thirty-six miles away and I had all day. The weather was bright with a strong cold wind from the north-east. A head-wind. Occasional snow flurries.

Here, it's worth taking some time to explain the problem of temperature control when on a bike. In cold weather, you need your layers. But the physical activity generates body heat and makes you sweat. Which evaporates and cools you down. And, once you're stationary, can make you very cold indeed. And then there's wind chill: it's much colder if you are moving. And you're always moving on a bike. And it's usually windy, to boot. You only have to look at a Met Office forecast to see the difference between mean air temperature and the "feels-like" temperature, when wind chill is factored in.

There's also the difference between dry cold and wet cold. In dry cold, especially if it's still, you can wear a T-shirt when it's ten below. For a while, anyway. It's the damp that conducts the chill into your bones. Same goes for humidity and heat. And if there's one commodity we have in abundance, it's damp.

I was layered up for the cold. On top was a fleece. But I sweated like a horse, especially when climbing up the long drags, and Lord knows there was plenty of that. If I took anything off, the razor wind sliced through my ribs and stripped out any heat being generated. Especially on a fast descent. I ended up with my Gore-Tex jacket on top as a windbreak. As Eliot has it, "Between melting and freezing, the soul's sap quivers."

At least the roads were quiet. Barely a vehicle passed. Occasional vans heading for some village. The houses, well maintained, appeared uninhabited. No human beings. Silence.

Routinely bolted on to the term Outer Hebrides is the adjective "remote". It's almost obligatory. It defines us. Do you have electricity there? Do you have running water? And yet, with an airport, ferry services, a critical mass of population and a diverse economy – including weaving, fishing, tourism, services – Lewis seemed positively metropolitan compared to the vast, desolate, silent swathes of Sutherland I passed through.

I took time to take a detour to the Coigach peninsula and, in late afternoon with the sweat rapidly cooling, arrived at the Culag. That evening, I had the traditional Highland hotel bar fare of fish and chips and peas and ran over the next day's route towards Kinlochbervie. I noticed a great many road-gradient arrow symbols were along the way on my planned route. A single arrow meant a gradient of between 14% and 20% (1 in 7), and a double arrow a gradient in excess of 20% (1 in 5). There were a lot.

I've subsequently seen that stretch of road referred to as the hilliest route in Britain.

Along this corrugated profile I came to experience the biological equivalent of metal fatigue. Lung-bursting climb after perpendicular climb sapped me and soaked me. They kept coming at me like waves of rock and on each one I left something of myself behind. The descents didn't allow recovery because of hairpin cornering and steepness. The risk of flying over a cliff edge or hitting a sheep or running head-on into an oncoming car. Constant braking. Even descending was hard work: the sweat lashed off me, vaporising in the cold restless air.

I had counted the arrowheads since Lochinver and chalked them off while psychologically preparing myself, rationing my effort, for the doubles. I took a detour to the lighthouse and somewhere along the spiking cardiograph of my progress, took comfort from the fact that the Drumbeg Hotel was coming up.

Next stop. Seldom was a rest, food and reboot so well deserved. Thanks be to God it was open. Only it wasn't. It was shut. It was so emphatically shut that nobody had even bothered taking down the "Open" sign six months ago.

Bitter, thwarted, through gritted teeth I yo-yoed along the road until, at last, at the top of an excruciating grovel up a long coil of tarmac, I chalked off my last double arrow. Shortly I would rejoin the main road. Maybe there would be something open at Kylesku.

As my heart rate began to drop below 200 beats per minute, I planned ahead for life on a more level playing field, and thought about what my ETA might be at KLB. Then I came across a road sign advising lorries to get into low gear and to check their brakes. Confused, I carried on until I pulled up roadside at what felt like the top of a steep cliff. Below me, the road plummeted away, only to rise again in a swooping ski-slope up the other side. I had miscalculated.

I ate a Mars Bar. I owed myself that much. At the bottom of the climb I dropped into the lowest gear I had. Even so, I had to stand out of the saddle to move forward. Halfway up, a car came behind me and as I moved to the side of the road I lost traction and my rear wheel spun on the fine loose gravel. Like a hamster on a wheel for those few seconds, I pedalled furiously, poised stationary, until I was able to move into the middle of the road again and inch my way to the top.

On this brisk, bitterly cold, dry day, soaked with sweat, I could not have been wetter if I had fallen in a river.

Under the bridge at Kylesku, there was a small hostelry of some kind. Fish and chips and peas. A period of reflection. Perhaps apprehension. It had been a brutal morning and the worst was certainly over in terms of difficulty. But I wasn't even halfway to my destination.

The climbs from then on were not as steep but, to make up

for it, they were longer. They were also into the sharp teeth of a sub-arctic headwind. Towards late afternoon, I turned left for the few miles along the rollercoaster to Kinlochbervie. I'd never been there so it only existed in my imagination as a port, probably a deal smaller than Ullapool, perhaps of a size with Lochinver, a seafront of shops and basic services backed up with some residential. Good enough, it would do. In fact, it seemed to comprise only of one enormous pier with industrial marine processing sheds and a handful of houses. Up another hill was the hotel. A modern system-built, box-with-a-roof just plonked down there. Any other time I might have been disappointed. Hoped for something with a bit more history, tradition, character. Not this time. It might as well have been Claridges.

By now I was everything you don't want to be on a bike: petrified with cold, wet, tired to the point of exhaustion, hungry enough to eat boiled grass. Probably dehydrated. I went inside. It was empty, so I rang the bell at reception. Eventually, a woman appeared who seemed startled to see a person standing there. I asked her if I could have a room, and she said, "Oh." She didn't know. They didn't usually bother opening at this time of year. She would have to wait for her husband. So I sat on the carpeted stair, hopelessly, and waited. "What if he says no?" I wondered. "I'll have to go round knocking on people's doors, begging."

The husband came in, glanced over at me and, given the basics, just said "Uuuuuh, yeah, I suppose so. Just the one night?"

In my room I ran the very hottest bath I could. Neat hot water, no cold to dilute. My layers peeled off like so much wet wallpaper. And I lowered myself into the deep cauldron. It was just shy of boiling and yet as I lay there, the gooseflesh on my legs stubbornly refused to go away. My testicles had shrivelled, inverted, retreated into my body. I had the supernatural experience of being in water so hot that I might ordinarily self-cook, while simultaneously feeling as cold as a raw prawn. I just could not warm up.

Much later I learned that what I had done could have induced a crash in my core temperature and that I might have lost consciousness and drowned in the bath. In which case, I might indeed have cooked.

That night, I went down to the public bar and had fish and chips and peas. Later, I watched Nottingham Forest playing in the UEFA Cup on the telly in my room. I really needed to rethink what I was doing here and what I had let myself in for. I needed to take stock.

Next day was a short hop up the road to Durness. Twenty miles or so. I hunkered down there and spend most of the day recovering. I toyed with the idea of going to Cape Wrath. And chucked that when I saw that it involved a boat trip and an eleven-mile cycle to reach the Cape. Anyway, there was no sign of a boat.

The next leg was along to Tongue or Bettyhill and then head for Lairg across the Flow Country, the largest area of wilderness in the UK. During those seventy-odd miles – most of which were across an empty, wind-scoured, snow-flecked silence, angled into the relentless wind – it seemed I passed no more than a dozen or so cars. No more than one crossing the Strath.

What happened in Lairg? Pass. I suppose I had fish and chips and peas again that night. My landlord turned out to have been the original manager in the Caberfeidh Hotel in Stornoway when it opened in the Seventies.

The fifty-mile stretch from Lairg back to Ullapool was wind-assisted and when I got there I decided to stay overnight and get the ferry the following day, which was Saturday.

Aftermath: Death Warmed Up

Next Monday, I was back at work. I was feeling a bit chewed up, depleted by the whole experience. As a training exercise, though, it was a serious shift now safely stored in my body bank. There was a board meeting that night but I phoned from home to say that I was off-colour. Couldn't make it. My throat was quite sore. I took to my bed. An early night. Nip it in the bud. I also resolved to take the following day off.

I come from a long, non-complaining tradition where attending a doctor is usually a last resort. Probably a death-bed visit. But after taking to my bed my condition nosedived and by Wednesday morning I was asking my brother to call the doctor. Which I'd never done before. I was that desperate. In bed, I overheard the conversation and dragged myself to the top of the stair. My brother turned and said, "They're asking if it's urgent." I said, "Well, no, it's not *urgent* but I don't want it to be ages before anyone comes," and went back to bed. And heard the muttered, muffled conversation continue.

Ten to fifteen minutes later, I became aware of voices and activity down in the living room. The doctor was there. I somehow got into my robe and slippers and shambled downstairs. Doctor Wilson was standing in the middle of the room in his coat, leather bag in hand, breathing sharply as if he had been running over the fields. "I heard it was urgent," he said, panting. "What's the trouble?" And I heard myself say, "Well, I've got a sore throat." And saw him mentally count to ten. Then he said, "Right. Let's take a look, shall we?"

He shone a torch down my throat and told me it was very red. But that was a good sign. It showed my body was fighting the infection. I'd never taken antibiotics and said I wasn't keen to start if it wasn't necessary. "No, no, no. Just ensure that you get lots of rest and lots of fluids." And that was it. I didn't feel any better but I suppose I felt reassured.

As he closed the door behind him, I wondered how I was supposed to get these fluids, seeing as a teaspoon of water down my throat felt like neat sulphuric acid. If I'd been offered morphine, I'd have taken it. Still, there it was, I'd just have to weather it out.

Now the days contracted to a perpetual night as the infection passed down my throat and into my lungs. I coughed and expectorated into a plastic bag beside the bed. A foul, gelatinous, black and green residue. My brother winced at the stench of decay when he came into my room. I couldn't decide as to whether I had a septic throat or pneumonia. Or both. Only when thirst tipped over into desperation was I able to force a drink down my throat through the noose of pain. My 40th birthday came and the diving club had a do arranged for me in the pub. Which was abandoned. I celebrated by managing to swallow a spoonful of yoghurt.

Now the thought came that this was it. That I wouldn't recover. The trajectory was inexorably down. My condition had been flatlining, at best, before dropping step-by-step and deteriorating down a flight of stairs into a cellar. I looked down the long black hole.

I didn't know what more to do. After the debacle of the previous home visit, I couldn't call a doctor anymore. I'd burned my bridges. Cried wolf. By now, that episode would have entered the annals of farcical anecdotes that emerge through the media from time to time to illustrate the fickleness and moronic sense of entitlement of the Great British Public. Like calling 999 because you can't find the tin-opener.

"And so" – I could hear the doctor tell his colleagues in the staff room – "I floored it and burst through the door, ready to perform CPR and get the paramedics on site. And then he told me he had a sore throat!" Ha ha ha. "Unbelievable. That's a good one, Martin. Did you actually call an ambulance or just prescribe him a Lemsip? I remember a time when I..."

Desperate times call for desperate measures. I needed that last resort: a second opinion. My chairman at the time was a GP, the pseudonym-ish Dr John Smith. Although I wasn't one of his patients, we were closely associated. He took one look and wrote me a prescription for antibiotics. It's as well we got on. I could think of previous chairmen who would have been happy to see me die, ideally in great pain, and then thrown a party.

I barely managed to swallow the first one. Excruciatingly, the crunched fragments shredded the lining of my throat. It was the first solid food to pass through that ring of fire for over a week. A day or two later, not quickly enough, I began to notice a perceptible, recognisable improvement. I had begun to think of the infection as being the size of a dinner plate. Over the days, it shrank to the size of a saucer, then a coaster and penultimately to a small coin. And then I envisaged it as an internal blister that I could locate at a precise location inside my throat. Until, like a cold sore, it vanished.

A few days later, I went back to work. Depending on your point of view, I was fashionably – enviably – lean and trim. Or, alternatively, emaciated. A while later, I got back on the bike.

Eden in the Morning

"There's someone coming," I said. "There's a car on the machair."
I looked at Em and said, "It'll be him. It'll be him. I told you, I
bloody told you he'd check." Em said, "Shut up. Where? No way.
He never checks." She looked through the narrow split in the
drawn curtains in the caravan window. A dark blue Volvo estate
was slowly undulating its way over the shimmering grass and
flowers towards us.

It was a Saturday morning in July, early enough for the machair
to be still damp with dew. We'd only been there a night. I'd been in
the bunk-bed when I first heard the engine. I noticed because the
sound didn't recede, it got louder.

Em was already up. She wasn't paying attention. Rummaging
in her bag. Hadn't yet bothered getting dressed. Well, she had
better get her kit on pretty damn quick.

There was no doubt. It was him. Doctor Grieve. Our landlord for the weekend. Em knew him through being a patient in
his practice during the couple of years she lived in Harris. She'd
cleaned house for him. Still knew him just well enough to ask if
she could stay in his caravan sometime. By herself, obviously, otherwise there would have been no point in asking. Not without a
wedding ring on her finger.

"Remember Lot's wife," he had said when he took his family
from their enclave in the Midlands to head for the Hebrides all
those years ago. To a place where there was still some decency left
to protect and conserve. Like a theological national park. A kind
of Eden unscathed by moral collapse. Where better?

There was less than a minute to react. Em was already dressed.
I'd never seen her do it so fast. Still haven't. The situation hadn't

so much unfolded as fallen on us like a collapsed roof. I had two options. Get dressed and try to act normal, or hide under the duvet, flatten out, throw some stuff on top and hope he wouldn't spot me.

No chance. Not with all my gear lying about. It was bloody obvious she wasn't alone. I could see him pulling the duvet off. Me underneath. Naked. Mortified. It didn't even bear thinking about. What a fucking farce. Christ, I was thirty-eight years old. And Em wasn't his daughter or his wife.

But she wasn't my wife, either.

I jumped into last night's shorts, scrambled a T-shirt, grabbed my paperback of *The Crow Road* and desperately threw myself into a sprawling, casual, been-up-for-a-while pose along the bench-seating at the other end of the caravan.

As a pre-emptive measure, Em had already gone out and I could now hear them talking. Sounded amicable enough. Couldn't make it out. Pleasantries. Maybe it would be okay. Maybe he wouldn't look in.

But he did. The door opened. Em said, "Roddy, this is Dr Grieve." I raised my eyes lazily from the book and said, "Morning. It looks like it's going to be a nice day." It really was as lame and phoney as that. My voice sounded like it was coming out of an old transistor radio.

There was eye contact for a frozen fraction of a second. The moment expanded. And petrified.

Later, when replaying the encounter, we were unable to recall anything that was said or happened within that blank space. It was like we'd had a spontaneous black-out. I think he wore a khaki waistcoat. With pockets. But I'm not sure.

The next thing I did remember was Em's voice coming through the open door. She was saying, "I'm so sorry, I didn't mean to…" He said something about being disappointed, that he was an old-fashioned sort and how he felt let down and expected better. And then, just when I thought he was going to leave it at that, the cheerless incantation went on. How he'd misjudged her. A betrayal of trust.

It brought to mind a Victorian dad thrashing his kids. More in sorrow than in anger. For your own good. One day, you'll thank me. This hurts me more than it hurts you.

It sure was old school. And it took me right back to it.

He didn't even have to say we needed to leave.

When the car door shut and the engine sound faded away, Em came back in. She looked wrecked, drained, beaten. She said, "We have to go." I said, "I know." She slumped down beside me on the bench-seat and we sat with our backs against the end window. Didn't say anything else. It felt like we'd been ambushed, ransacked.

I had glazed over. I was looking vacantly towards the other end of the caravan where, barely five minutes earlier, I had lain in a woolly-headed, semi-conscious cocoon.

I became aware that I was staring at something under the bed. Last night's bed. An object. No. "Jesus, Em," I said. "There's a dead bird under there." A glimpse of iridescence. "It's... a starling. How come we didn't notice it till now?" I stood up, walked over and crouched down to investigate when, with another start, I saw that it was breathing. "It's alive," I said, turning round. "How is it alive? Did it come in during the night? The window wasn't open. Was the window open? How come we didn't hear it?"

But when I looked again, I saw that it wasn't alive. It was still moving, though. Its entire chest cavity was crammed with a seething, heaving colony of maggots.

For a second, I was sure I was going to retch.

I thought about leaving it where it was. Just ship out. Lock the windows, shut the door. Bottle it up. Let the larvae consume the host and ripen into a dense, black swarm of flies. So that when

Grieve returned the following weekend, he would find Beelzebub in residence.

But I didn't. I swallowed my disgust. I gripped a wingtip between thumb and forefinger, whipped the bird out and flicked it through the open door onto the lush, verdant machair.

Then I sat down again. And breathed. And put my head in my hands.

Soon the sun would grow and gather in brightness and heat. I went outside, shaded my eyes and looked across the brightly speckled grass towards the dazzling white sands, the turquoise water and the islands beyond. It was a rare, perfect day for the beach. That had been the plan.

Instead, I stuffed our gear into bags and put them in the car boot with our box of food and bottles of wine, while Em frenetically wrote out a letter of apology to Grieve in her sketchbook. It ran to three long pages and there wasn't much punctuation. Once written, it was never sent.

We headed back to Stornoway in silence.

Forty miles later, we sat opposite each other at the window in her first-floor flat watching the traffic and the usual Saturday people. More silence. Em said, "I'm going to make some coffee."

I looked at my watch. It was 9.37am.

Walking

Capri

My partner Moira's aunt married an Italian architect called Renato and spent almost all her happily married, adult life in Naples. They had what she always referred to as an *àirigh* on the island of Capri. Bought in the Sixties before lunatic prices shut the door on normal people. Suffice to say, though, it was not a dry-stone bee-hive with a turf roof, nor a corrugated iron shack. It was a decent house in the town of Anacapri. It had a garden with cherry and lemon trees, a couple of bedrooms and a roof terrace. The house was sited down a narrow, steep, jinking passageway from the town centre. Halfway was a corner called La Pausa, a brief level respite where you could get your breath back.

Capri is basically a mountain sticking out of the Mediterranean. The eponymous town is sited a third of the way up the slope and Anacapri is a few kilometres further up a corkscrewing road climb.

In the olden days, B.C. (before children), we were actually able to afford to take a holiday abroad. That said, all it took was a cheap flight. The idea that we might have managed a week's accommo-dation in this millionaire's playground was beyond preposterous.

Many restaurants in the town of Capri had photographs in their windows of famous customers dining on the premises. Not Italian soap stars either. Mostly Hollywood A-listers, bronzed and beaming, holding up glasses of *vino rosso* or *limoncello*. Dustin Hoffman, Sophia Loren, for example. High rollers. The main street was a parade of intimidating fashion shops that just dared you to enter. Come ahead, if you think you're rich enough.

Weirdly, the cheapest thing I bought there was a huge tumbler of Glen Grant whisky. When I went to settle up the barman told me the price in lira and I thought, "Fair enough, about £14. That would be about right, not bad given it's a single malt and the size of the measure. About a quarter pint. *And* it's Capri." But no no no, *signore...* it was only £4. A fraction of the price I'd have paid in the UK.

We did the usual things, eating and drinking, wandering and meandering. Nothing. I read Arthur Miller's autobiography, *Timebends*. We chalked off the must-sees: Axel Munthe's house, the Blue Grotto – where we swam illegally. One day, we took the ferry to Sorrento on the Amalfi coast to go to Pompeii, which was unsatisfactory because we spent most of the day getting there and getting back. We somehow hadn't twigged that this was more than a museum visit, it was an actual town-sized town, about the size of Stornoway. You really needed more than an hour and a half to see it. Which, perhaps, you could not say about Stornoway.

It was apparently the coldest June on record. Which, for me, translated into uncomfortably hot. We spent an entire day at a small rocky cove and anchorage called Fago. Popular with the locals. A blinding, paper-white figure among the leathery burnt-umber bodies basking like crocodiles on the pier, I didn't exactly fit in. But nobody seemed to notice or care. In the broiling heat, it was chilled. We sat, stunned in the lazy daze of that smitten afternoon. A far cry from the crammed, basted-seal colonies of most beaches on the Med.

Before the sun went over the yardarm and the excellent prospect of a Campari, an aperitif to the fresh tuna steaks that I'd bought at the fish market that morning, we would chalk off the 589-metre ascent of Mont Solaro, the highest point on the island. That translates as 1,866 feet but we were already most of the way there. There was a chair lift from Anacapri but – you know what? – let's just take the path. It won't take long, be good exercise, we'll see more, work up an appetite and take the chairlift down. We can even have a couple of beers at the observatory restaurant at the top to round off this perfect afternoon.

Moira wore a red striped A-line skirt, a light blue blouse and red leather ballet pumps. I was in shorts, GAP t-shirt and a pair of loafers.

It began well enough, a not-too-demanding incline. But, very quickly, the rocky path narrowed and steepened. It kinked and veered off to sheer, precipitous, dizzying cliff edges. Sections like a ridge walk. It began to feel dangerous. On this coldest of Capri Junes, the late afternoon sun beat down and radiated off the gravel and stone. Sticky sweat maps appeared on our clothes, front and back, like Rorschach inkblot tests. Lizards scuttled across our path, a snake one time; there was an intense, heady scent of rosemary, pine, lemon, and a high chitter of crickets to complete the sensory landscape.

By the time it began to tip over from uncomfortable to concerning, we had already tipped over into we-can't-turn-back-now territory. We'd come this far. Anyway, the prospect of going down was more alarming still. Far below, a dazzling white villa, with a swimming pool like a blue eye, offered a vertiginous perspective.

Our water ran out.

"This was your idea." "Look, we'll be heading inland, away from the cliff soon. We're nearly there. We're so nearly there. And we're taking the chairlift back down. Just concentrate on that cold beer. Think of it as training for a cold beer."

So we trekked on until, as had been rather shakily predicted, we arrived at the observatory at the top. It was shut. There would be no beer. Nor would there be a chairlift to take us down. Everything closed at five o'clock. There was not a soul to be seen anywhere.

"Look on the bright side," I said. "We can just go round the other side of the building and – here, on the map – there's a path straight down to Anacapri. It's a pain and a drag but at least it will be shorter, easier and – bonus points – impossible to get lost." Because just by going downhill we can't not arrive. It's not that big an island.

The map showed a few paths, actually, threading down the mountain. At least there would be no cliff-edge dramatics this time. Still, as we began to descend through trees, bush, brush and scrub, it was not as overwhelmingly obvious as it had appeared on paper. There was no road, landmark or feature to refer to, far less a signpost. On the dry dappled path, crowded by rustling foliage, there was no overview. Just follow the path. If you could call it a path.

The downer at the top had induced a sense of anxiety. Introduced a psychological factor. It had to be the only reason that it seemed to take so much longer to get down than get up. Just follow the path.

So we did, until the trees stopped and we arrived at what can only be described as a precipice. Cemented into the ground at the top was a metal pole from which trailed a chain, stanchioned intermittently, as it disappeared down the cliff face. There was no point in arguing, no point in finger-pointing, no point in looking for another option. There was no going back. This was the only option. We had to go over. We had to go down. We just had to fucking finish this. Take it to the end.

So we each grabbed the chain and, hand over hand, lowered ourselves down, bracing our legs against the descent. Until it began to level out. And then, finally, a road appeared. And then some houses. And then a town. But it wasn't Anacapri. It was Capri. Three kilometres past our target destination and a couple of hundred metres down the mountain.

We walked towards the town feeling like a pair of tramps transposed from some absurdist student production. Red-faced, scuffed, scratched, sheened with sweat and crusted with dust. Our shoes looked like they had come out of a cement mixer. As we approached, we had to stop and become an unwitting audience to an Italian wedding. Either that or a Dolce & Gabbana shoot. Or a reimagining of the opening scenes from *The Godfather*. The bride, groom and guests poised, posed for the photographer in front of a gorgeous, glossy, sun-glinted, cherry-red vintage Ferrari. Framed by the hierarchy of family, generations and tradition. Impeccably groomed, immaculately tailored suits, exquisite couture, shoes polished to a mirror-finish, button-holed with roses: It was like a fantasy, a quintessence of Italian style, elegance, elan and order. An image of a kind of paradise.

We looked down at our shoes. I had never felt so shabby.

After the pictures, eyes still lowered, we were able to shamble past and it crossed my mind that they might not even allow us to enter the town. That we would be lowering the tone. Undesirables. An embarrassment. There were standards to uphold, after all. Who could blame them?

But everyone just ignored us. There were, of course, much better things to look at. And so we got the bus skywards, all the way back up the mountain to Anacapri and the postponed beer.

Across Ross

Moira and I were having a weekend meal with my brother Iain. Quaffing wine. In a mellow mood. He was talking about a charity walk that he had done a couple of times, called Across Ross. What a great experience it was. It took place over a Saturday and Sunday in May and was literally an organised coast-to-coast trek across Scotland. From Dingwall in the east to Eilean Donan castle in the west. About sixty-five miles. You should do it, he said. He'd been in his T-shirt the whole time last year.

I said, "That's a hell of a distance over two days. Like walking from Stornoway to Tarbert in Harris and back." He shook his head emphatically, said it doesn't feel like it. There are food stops, stations, support; it's broken up into bite-sized chunks. It's not a race, you just do it in your own time. You should do it. "It's a doddle."

So, why not? I bought a decent pair of walking boots and got round to breaking them in, in the few weeks before the excursion. I wasn't going to fall for that one. Moira already had a pair of boots.

We booked a B&B in Dingwall, a sleepy small town. On the road to comatose, because, like a lot of Highland satellite towns, the commercial life has been sucked out of it by Inverness. The great retail and leisure vortex. We went for a curry the night before the *Grand Départ*, which was at 6am. Our gear would be put in a minibus, for collection at the end of the walk. It was a good system. But only if you remembered to take your holdall or rucksack with you to the start. Not leave it at the B&B, which is what Moira did. An omen in the gloamin'.

The morning was chilly, draughty and at the beginning merely overcast with spitting rain. We set off. A journey of sixty-five miles starts with a single step. My brother marched ahead into the distance.

It was indeed in chunks but it hadn't actually occurred to me that eight miles is quite a long way to walk. A couple of hours? And then repeat over variable terrain half a dozen times. Then get up and do it all over again. Okay, it's not a run, but it's still a couple of marathons with an additional fifteen miles' extra-time thrown in. Maybe not such "a piece of piss", after all.

And then there's the weather factor. Miles Kington once wrote a column questioning as to why, in Britain of all places, there was not the equivalent of a Beaufort Scale for rain, as there was for wind. And went on to suggest one, ranging from a barely perceptible dampness in the air to rain running *up* the windows, where a newspaper read on a park bench would turn to pulp in your hands. Hurricane-force rain.

What can I say of the weather visited upon us that memorable morning? A reliable signature of severity is when the ferries are cancelled. As they were. And that it was a freezing, gale-force wind from the north, mercifully (but only marginally) at our backs. The effect was like being trailed mile after mile by someone with a pressure-hose trained on you at full power.

I had a cycling jacket on, which had served me in good stead in extreme conditions. But it might as well have been made out of kitchen roll. Moira's showerproof cagoule was even more useless. Had I known what was ahead of me I might have worn neoprene.

An hour or so after we had passed the first stop, my feet were already beginning to hurt. I checked for blisters. None. Surprisingly. It just felt like it. It disturbed a dormant feeling from the juvenile Skye expedition, as if it were leaking out from the locked box in my head where I had consigned it. I began to understand why beating the soles of a prisoner's feet was such an effective and popular means of torture. There were long stretches along narrow, quiet roads and early on we gravitated to the soft verge. Preferable to the unrelenting smack and whack of tarmac. Moira had gone utterly silent. Never a good sign.

As a fairly serious cyclist, I was physically, aerobically, in good nick and I cannot say that at any time I was ever exhausted, or even very tired. It was the one punishment I was spared. But I was plodding with unconscious determination further and further away from my comfort zone.

The day assembled with a cabinet maker's precision into a compendium of misery. The cold, sopping wet and increasing foot pain, turbocharged by an interior, involuntary, unwelcome and intrusive litany of self-inflicted goading. Personal bulletins: "You're not even a quarter of the way yet." "This isn't going to get any less painful, you know, it's just going to get worse." "If it's this bad now, can you imagine what it will be like at the end?" "You can't force your way through this." Each signpost seemed to say, "Suffering 10 miles"; "More Suffering 25 miles"; "SUFFERING-on-Sea 40 miles" ... And so on, all the way to Hell-to-Pay.

The last section of the morning took us through a forest and to lunch at the Strathpeffer village hall. Adorned with stags' heads, I feel certain it's been featured in *Vogue*. It now resembled a prison camp. Moira was shaking so much in the toilet that she could barely get her clothes off. Plastered to her back. Stripped out of our wet gear, even the change of clothes in the rucksacks had to be dried in front of gas heaters. We ate hot food, gulped coffee and warmed up. The rain eased off. In an hour, morale had lifted: we weren't going to give up that easily. We were suited, booted, refuelled, ready to rock again.

It took about two minutes up the road for us to be jerked back to sure and sore reality, like a dog on a lead. Or, more morbidly, a hangman's drop.

By late afternoon, we were among the stragglers. Tail-end Charlies. The last section was ten miles off-road, following a river up the Strath to an overnight lodge. Crucially, from this point on there would be no support. No broom wagon to sweep us up if we wanted to quit. The support staff had been waiting for us to eventually appear at the penultimate stop of the day; they'd been monitoring our progress. Probably had an amber sticker against us, a red flag at the ready. They fussed a bit and interrogated us with benevolent concern. Did we really want to continue? Were we up to it? Did we realise that there would be no back-up from now on? If you carry on, we can't help, can't pick you up.

We looked on the positive side. There would be no more tarmac that day. The going would be softer underfoot. Also, quitting was not something that came easily or naturally.

So, stepping gingerly, we followed the river, fairly regularly crossing the little tributaries that fed into it from the high sur-rounding mountains. A couple of miles upriver, we met some Duke of Edinburgh Award students with their Group Leader. He told us that further up, a feeder stream was in spate and that they had only just managed to cross.

Shortly afterwards, we came to said stream. Evidently, there had been some dramatic exaggeration going on because we waded across easily, at the expense of little more than wet feet. By now, a steely commitment had set in; the end of the day was in sight. Food, sleep, maybe even a drink.

So we continued up the river. And stopped. In front of us a downsized thundering Niagara disgorged into the river. It was impossible. Impassable. But if we followed it up the mountain, there would be less volume and we might be able to cross. We climbed for half a mile and still couldn't do it. Back down by the river the last few stragglers had now bunched up by the torrent. Among them an older, evidently more experienced walker took charge and determined that we could find a shallower shoal of the main river downstream and could cross by linking arms in a human chain. What else could we do? Damned if *I* know.

When we found a stretch we followed instructions and braced, leaning, waist-deep in the powerful current and strung our way to the other side. More a cheap necklace than a human chain. Now we had to find a place further upstream to re-cross the river to the same side as the lodge. This second crossing was narrower and deeper. The water at chest height, more urgent.

Coming up to nine o'clock, in near darkness and to the strains of a piper, we arrived at the lodge. By then, most of the walk-ers who had arrived were already asleep. Gallingly, my brother looked as if he had been crashed out for at least a couple of hours. We got some food, a dram, took our boots off and stuffed them with newspaper in front of the guttering fire.

There was no floor space left at ground level, so we went upstairs. I had an inflatable mattress and blew it up. As I crawled into my sleeping bag I could simultaneously feel it deflate to the hard wooden floor. But I wasn't moving anymore that night. Around us in the darkness, an atonal symphony of farting emanated from the scattered bodies, similarly deflating.

Next morning was a five o'clock start. We got into our cold wet boots and were among the last to leave. We could barely stand, far less walk. We would have to acclimatise to the pain afresh. In half an hour we were fording a river on a rope bridge, then ascending a zig-zag mountain stairway and a high pass. At least it was dry.

The first stop was at a gamekeeper's lodge several miles over this mountain pass. I like a drink, but I had never had a large whisky at ten o'clock on a Sunday morning. On the other hand, I had never felt the need. I didn't actually live in a Country & Western song. What else? Yes, venison burgers. And a foot massage. Later on, there was another major river crossing, facilitated by a digger. We sat in the scoop. I mustn't forget the highlights.

Towards the end of the afternoon, we passed the last checkpoint. "Congratulations, you're almost there," they said. "Almost there" was another eight miles, mostly on the main road to Eilean Donan castle. Hello tarmac, my old friend. It felt more like eighty miles. It was the hardest stretch of the whole two days.

The three of us fell asleep instantly on the bus to Inverness. We got a B&B. I nearly got run over the following morning, on account of the painfully slow pace of my hobble across the road. It took me three days before I could walk normally again.

The Key

It's not just me.

My brother Iain got a phone call while we were out on the Coll moor cutting peats. "Uh-huh... uh-huh... okay... How did it happen?... Okay, tell me later... Yeah, I'll come down when I get home. It'll be about an hour."

He looked at me and rolled his eyes. "Munro," he said. "They're down at Gress and the car won't start. He wants me to come and tow it with the tractor."

"*Tractor*?" I said. "Jesus, can they not just get jump-leads or a push?" He shook his head. "I don't know. Sounds more complicated than that."

It was.

Munro was in my year at school and became a senior manager in a global eye-surgery business. He had married Juliette, a Dutch-ess – in that she was Dutch – and they lived in the Netherlands. Every summer, the family, including three enormously tall boys and Jock the German dachshund, decanted to Munro's family home in Lewis in a Chrysler space-wagon loaded to the gunnels. Much of it fishing gear. Zeebrugge to Hull, then the long drive to north-west Scotland and another ferry to Stornoway. Took a couple of days but they usually stayed for three or four weeks.

This was the third last day of their holiday before they headed back to the Continent.

What happened is that they were down at Gress beach, about a mile from our house, when, on this clear-blue-sky summer's day, middle-boy-Munro (MBM), said he'd left something in the car. Munro gave him the key and carried on reading. And on his way back MBM dropped the key by accident into a shallow rock pool.

It was only for a couple of seconds. He shook it dry, wiped it on his shorts and gave it back to his dad.

Later that afternoon, when they returned to the car and pressed the key to open the door, it didn't work. They were locked out. And when they eventually did get inside, with police assistance, they found the car was unresponsive. In fact, completely immobilised.

Another phone call and Juliette and the boys crammed into a taxi to take them home. Munro waited. Iain chugged down with the tractor, the low-tech diesel mule that was to effect the rescue. After some shunting and dragging round, he was able to hitch it on and towed the inert vehicle at 15mph to Munro's house in Laxdale, which was about six miles or so. Where things could be sorted out.

Needs must. The key was blow-dried with a hairdryer and then put in a very, very low oven. Which made no difference. Nothing worked. Nothing bloody worked.

There was nothing for it, he had to phone his father-in-law in Holland and ask him to send the spare key. If he could find it. Which he couldn't. Until, eventually, he could. He'd had to leave work and travel from an outlying town into Amsterdam to do so. That took six hours. It would need to be sent immediately, next-day international delivery by DHL, if they were going to make their deadline. There was a tracking number.

But it did not arrive the next day. The key was locked somewhere in the digital ether.

So, in the meantime, Munro phoned the only Chrysler dealer in the north of Scotland and explained the situation. There was abundant sympathy but, with hindsight, he had suffered from a lack of foresight: "If you'd phoned a couple of weeks earlier, we could have done something, but that model has been discontinued. It's no longer on the system."

Now the realisation began to assert itself that they might have to fly home. But then, how would they get the car back if there was no one to drive it? The situation, by each calculation, was becoming more complex – as well as beginning to declare itself in stark monetary terms.

Metaphorically, the car was a taxi. And they were stuck inside it, in a traffic jam with the meter running on their way to an unavoidable, critical hospital appointment.

Exasperating, but – in the end – obviously an insurance job. Cut and dried. Only, the car's insurance brokers, while sympathetic, were unwilling to be convinced: it was an unusual problem; they would need to check the terms and conditions; technically, the car is operational, not "damaged"; in a sense, it is not so different to having a flat battery, or running out of petrol, or just having lost your key. Have you contacted a garage? We have no evidence that the car is disabled, etc. Have you contacted the dealers? It seems to us more of a travel insurance issue. It was difficult to reason with them.

Still the key did not arrive.

By now, the prospect and process of cancelling the ferry bookings came into play. It was unclear as to whether a refund could be claimed at such short notice. And flights had to be booked. Miraculously, there were seats available the day after they'd been scheduled to leave, at a hefty price. Especially as they had to pay the fully-flexible premium because – y'know – the seats might not be needed because the spare key might still arrive.

But it didn't. From the tracking, though, it appeared to have arrived in Inverness.

At this juncture, the prevailing image is of an emptying egg timer. Time accelerating and the matter funnelling into crisis. Logistically, they had so much stuff that they would have to load most of it into the car anyway and leave it. So they did. The phone bill to the insurance and the travel companies grew. Flourished.

Then. Push came to shove. Decision time. They would have to

take the flights. The options had narrowed too much. They would leave the next day.

The following morning, two taxis arrived and took them to the airport, heavily laden. They took their place in the queue for check-in and, in due course, lugged their luggage onto the conveyor belt. Jock was on a lead, probably the most relaxed member of the troupe. Big mistake.

Because the attendant said, "You can't take that dog onto the flight. It'll have to go in the hold. But you'll still need to put it in a box." Munro said, "We don't have a box." Guy said, "I'm really sorry, sir, but that's just the rules."

So there was a frantic phone call to his brother who was still at home: "Is there a box? Find a box, anything big enough with four sides and... a lid... and... and... phone a taxi before you even start looking... and tell him to fucking floor it to the airport..."

Maybe twenty minutes later the taxi screeched up at the airport with a battered old cat box. Maybe, *maybe*, just big enough. But the prospect of poor Jock in the hold inspired some creative thinking. Along with the box, Munro's brother had inexplicably thrown in an old Adidas sports bag. So Juliette did a number on the attendant, who finally relented and said, "Okay, okay, but you have to make sure he stays there." So Jock was put in the sports bag, with his head poking out, and was allowed on the flight as hand luggage. They slumped into their seats and as the plane took off their spirits lifted. Nobody spoke.

The next day, the key arrived. His brother put it in a padded envelope and sent it straight back to Holland.

A couple of weeks later, the Chrysler arrived. On the back of a flat-bed lorry.

In Memoriam Jock, 2001–2017

Mole

Once you've got out past the breakers to open water and find yourself in a stable, long-term relationship, some of the bigger issues start to assert themselves. These tend to come under the broad umbrella of reproduction.

Men can be broody, too. But I got pretty much over it in my thirties. Leaving no genetic footprint on the earth didn't really bother me after that. It was a clever move because, of course, as soon as you are no longer interested, you can be certain that you will get what you no longer want.

The pursuit of a future partner can be a definition of futility and frustration. One such time I did everything I could, and in reward found myself precisely nowhere, depressed, drained and exhausted. Ignored. Literally hope-less. Either she really wasn't interested or she got a kick from the hold she had over me. It was kind of humbling.

Nothing made any difference. Nothing, that is, except nothing. Doing nothing. I gave up. Moved on. Forgot about her. Forced myself to at least try. And one day she simply presented herself. Came to see me. Later she confessed that she'd heard through a friend that I'd abandoned hope and had felt a pang of hurt and regret. Had even felt a little offended. It made her realise how she really felt. Shortly after, she discovered that she had been right the first time. And we both moved on, in opposite directions. Thus we learn.

I never properly understood the concept of "trying for a baby". Outwith IVF, of course. You could certainly try *not* to have a baby by implementing certain methods. Physical intervention. Contraception. Otherwise, assuming there were no issues, wasn't a child just an eventual by-product of a normal, functioning, healthy, fully-fledged relationship?

So Moira and I didn't try. Successfully. She became pregnant.

Some things within the female sphere of a relationship seem permanently below the radar. PMT is just joke-fodder. Although it's hard to see the funny side when a partner becomes violently psychotic each full moon. Domestic lycanthropy. Perhaps it's where the origin story lies.

The menopause can have debilitating symptoms and be a kind of bereavement for some women. And then there's miscarriage.

I can't say I really understood what it meant. Until Moira miscarried. I got a text: *Can you come round now?* The ultrasound had shown that there was no heartbeat. An evacuation procedure would have to be performed the next day. The definition: natural spontaneous abortion. "Pregnancy loss" didn't seem to cover it. Facts were not enough.

As you were. We would need to go back to not wanting it all over again. After adjusting and recalibrating to meet this new future, there it was, Gone. *How Ya Gonna Keep 'Em Down on the Farm (After They've Seen Paree)?*

And then, like we had joined a secret society, it seemed as if every couple we knew, or every other mother at least, had been through it. Seldom did something so "abnormal" become so normalised.

So we continued not trying. And a couple of years on, a late period became two blue lines. The Blue Period – since we're artists. And history duly repeated itself. No heartbeat in the first trimester. Down the snake. Throw a six to start again.

Did we get used to it? I can't say. I suppose so; there was plenty other stuff to be getting on with. It's not a human right to have a child. Despite the soothing reassurances from the medical profession – it's common, it's natural, it's normal – all the empirical evidence suggested that it just wasn't going to happen. And, in a way, that was okay. Nobody's fault.

Third time lucky? Part of me was pleased, part of me must have thought, "Here we go again." I had transited from my original naïve assumption that once pregnant, short of a termination or falling down a flight of stairs, it would conclude with a guaranteed delivery. That it was inevitable. Now I thought of the fragile cluster of cells as a teetering Jenga tower.

On a Monday morning in January, before work, apprehensively, we both turned up for the first scan. Let's get it over with. But lo! A blurry shape and a heartbeat like a jackhammer. It wasn't like the other two times, after all.

The gynaecologist – a brusque Middle Eastern woman – seemed preoccupied however, perhaps a little concerned. There was a shadow on the ultrasound. And she and the assistant nurse were having an under-the-breath, coded half-conversation as she manoeuvred the scanner over Moira's jellied belly. It might be a blood clot. We would need to see if it had abated in a week's time. Or it might be a partial mole.

The only question I asked was, "Is this anything we should be worried about?" I was told that they would just need to monitor it and see how things turned out.

I went to work, determined not to look it up. Not to ruin my day. But resistance was futile. I read on Wikipedia that "molar pregnancy is an abnormal form of pregnancy which… will fail to come to term... a gestational trophoblastic disease which grows into a mass in the uterus that has swollen chorionic villi… Molar pregnancies are categorised as partial moles or complete moles, with the word *mole* being used to denote simply a clump of growing tissue, or a *growth*."

There was much additional stuff about chromosomal abnormality, yoked to the possibility that if the growth was malignant, chemotherapy would be required and another pregnancy impossible for a further year after treatment.

It was worse than a miscarriage. But we refused to catastrophise until everything was confirmed. Moira sounded upbeat on the phone. Her friend Xaviere, whose mother was a midwife, said it was extremely rare and the thing to hang on to was that there was a heartbeat. That was all that mattered.

About six o'clock on Thursday evening, the phone rang. It was the hospital. "Could I speak to Moira?" Who's calling? "Anne." Just that. No more information. The conversation would need to be with the intended recipient alone. Moira was upstairs in bed. Exhausted. She was sleeping a lot. I took the cordless phone, gave it to her and left the room. Five minutes later, I went back up. She was in bits. It had been confirmed.

Next day, as if to underscore the diagnosis, there was a minor discharge of blood. Spotting. On Sunday, just to get out of the house, we drove to the village of Tolsta Chaolais and, without conscious intention, parked beside the house used for the children's TV programme *Katie Morag*. The dark, squally, bitter January weather in close harmony with our mood. We resolved to just get on with it. Get through it. Get it over with. Fuck it, what else could we do? What worse could happen now?

That next Monday, the shadow remained. Whatever sun was casting it, nothing had changed in that firmament. But for all the weight of evidence, there was yet a scintilla of doubt that stopped it a hair's breadth short of definitive. A few days later, our consultant called Moira in and told her that she could take her into theatre for an evacuation right now. Or, she could send her to the Queen Mother's Hospital in Glasgow for a scan. They had more advanced sonographic equipment there so it would be conclusive. A second opinion. There was an unspoken sense that it was a waste of time but at least due process would be served. "It's your choice." So she opted for the second scan. The appointment was over a month away.

Around that time we ran a series of evening talks by artists, called *Art After Dark*. One of the first was by the acclaimed sculptor Steve Dilworth, and Moira went along. At the start of his talk, Steve passed round a fertility goddess figurine, the Venus of Willendorf, referencing it as an influence on his work and how it represented origins, both historic and symbolic. It's primal absoluteness. It's uncompromised purity. You can't be half-pregnant.

Moira's heart crumpled. She thought, "But isn't that what I am?"

So we served out our sentence in this no man's, no hope, shadow-land. Stranded, as Shakespeare would have it, "between the acting of a dreadful thing and the first motion" where "all the interim is like... a hideous dream". Only after Glasgow could we get on with getting on with it.

Moira had a shared shop-cum-studio on a corner of Church Street. It hadn't taken more than a few months though to figure out that, with rent, business rates, electricity and stock, it was a non-starter. A really good week might have covered the bills. Paying herself a modest wage? Forget it. So that was something to do in the meantime, to take our minds off things: shut down, pack up and ship out.

She was due to go out on the early flight but it wasn't clear as to whether she would have to overnight it after the operation. A late afternoon return flight had been booked but it could be changed. That morning, I set about emptying the small shop of the trappings of the failed little business. How ironic. How morbidly appropriate.

Then, sometime towards noon, while driving with a load for the dump, my phone rang and I turned into a side street and pulled over. Moira. Here it comes. I said, "How are you, what did they say, what's going to happen?" She said, "Umm, well, they told me I'm normal." I was speechless. What? It wasn't the last thing I'd expected because it wasn't even on that list.

Eventually I said, "What do you mean, 'normal'? How can you be normal?" I couldn't find it in myself to feel happy or relieved about it. Couldn't summon it. Wasn't prepared. Couldn't adjust. I couldn't reach that far up or bridge that distance yet. If anything, I felt frustrated, disorientated. Also, weirdly, like I'd been ambushed. Or tricked.

"Apparently, it's just a thickening of the womb wall. The nurse said to me, 'Don't be too disappointed. You thought you were special, didn't you?' Then she asked me for my book and I gave her the little notebook I always carry and she said, 'NO. Your BOOK! Did they no' give you a book?' I said no."

The book she was referring to was a maternity logbook. We'd been given nothing but a desolate prognosis. Next time we attended the hospital we left heavily laden with tote-bags stuffed with books, leaflets, pamphlets, T-shirts, bibs, stickers, mugs... It was now official: we were going to have a baby.

At the next consultation we were asked if we wanted an amniocentesis in the second trimester. This involves taking spinal fluid from the foetus to determine the probability of Down's syndrome. If positive, it would give us the option to terminate. One of the side effects of an amnio is that it marginally increases the chance of miscarriage. By then, we'd already had enough. We said no.

A little knowledge is a dangerous thing. Afterwards, I wondered if we would have been better off never knowing in the first place. The outcome would have been the same and we would not have had to negotiate that gruelling psychological assault course. Or come within a heartbeat of inadvertently terminating our own and our daughter's unlived life.

At 7am on the 2nd of October, 2009, in the routine agony of childbirth, Iris Isabella was delivered in perfect health, weighing seven pounds and eleven ounces. Mother and baby both well.

It was also the day of Moira's wedding anniversary. But not mine.

Potato Syndrome

It was a routine get-together. Usual crew, sitting in The Crown with pints. Thursday night at the end of the month. Pay day. Usual subjects, football, work, schools, kids, holidays – nothing contentious, ever – always defaulting to the lowest common denominator. The glue that bound us. I was always good at dull.

Mortgages and house prices were a favourite topic. Everybody had their own story, like a party piece. A shared misery or a minor triumph. How they'd got more, or less, for their property. Interest rates, fixed-term loans, how these guys pulled out of the deal, how there was a feeding frenzy round this house. Or how the Crofting Commission held the whole thing up for nine fucking months (Jon E's story. Again.) There was a comforting choreography to it. Line-dancing our scripted lives.

The new homeowner in our little group was called Colin. Collie-Dog, we called him, on account of our chronic lack of imagination. And because, maybe, if you made something up, he seemed so attentive. Only just joined our elite squad and we hadn't heard from him yet. Not that we were interested. The only story anyone wanted to hear was their own.

But still. Better get it over with. "How was it for you, Colin?"

"Not so good. But it turned out well in the end."

"Yeah? How was that?"

"Well, we'd had the offer accepted on the new property. In town. And so we sold our house – not for the price we wanted, but we needed the money. It had to be a quick sale because we had a tight deadline to get out. Then we ended up in a chain and the Crofting Commission got involved…"

Much eye-rolling and sympathetic muttering about these

clowns and their Dickensian practices. "Maybe you need something stronger than a pint, Colin," said Billy Stripe. Much chortling.

Anyway, so far so utterly standard, though it did get marginally more entertaining – if that's the right word – as he trowelled on the misery. Their buyer was a bitch-from-hell who screwed them into the ground. She needed to get into the house pronto and so they got turfed out and were drifters for six months before they could get into the new property. Homeless with three small kids, four cats and a dog. Oh yeah, and a fish-tank. Being processed through the legal sausage machine. There was a short spell with his sister in her one-bedroom flat, before that got well beyond unbearable. The cats had let it be known what they thought of it by using his sister's backpack as a litter tray.

Then renting some dump on Seaforth Road at eye-watering prices. Then, when they at last got into the house, there were so many problems that it was like it had been booby-trapped. And then the money ran out.

It was hard not to sympathise but in the end, y'know, who cares? We let him carry on. Fair enough though, I thought, he's had it worse than any of us.

But I didn't have all night. So I said, "That's bad craic, Colin, but what's the happy ending here?"

His posture relaxed and his face loosened and lit up as if a fond memory had been summoned.

It's a bit much to say that there was great expectation round the table, but at least we were heading towards some sort of conclusion. Must have had a windfall, come into money, I thought. Dead uncle. Something like that.

Anyway, buoyed by whatever-it-was, he went on: "It was a few weeks in and we'd just got the gas cooker working so we didn't have to eat out or live on takeaways. I decided to make a meal to celebrate. I'd bought all the stuff…" And he proceeded to relate the entire shopping list. I could rattle it off, but do you really want to know why he always buys long-grain instead of basmati rice, and his strongly held views on tomato sauce? Didn't think so.

It was hard to see where exactly it was all going but, given the level of detail and what you could only call momentum, it had to be significant. Surely not some heartwarming, pointless yarn about the first dinner he'd ever made in his new house. So, to prevent that, and in an attempt to move things on, I said, "Yep, Colin, a good meal can make you see things very differently."

"You're dead right there," he said. "But it wasn't that."

He went on: "I'd bought a sack of Maris Pipers and thought I'd make a big pan of mash to go along. But I couldn't find the potato-peeler we had. It must have been in some box or other, waiting to be unpacked. So – just on the off-chance – I looked in the drawer. And one was there! Left behind."

Billy Stripe, Jon E and Alec didn't react. Their faces were kind of glazed and blank. Cream Soda was giving me a sideways look.

"It was stainless steel and had a round handle with a bit of black plastic trim. It looked handy so I emptied the bag of spuds into the sink, grabbed it and just got stuck in. Oh man, it was unbelievable. I stripped those babies in a couple of minutes. I remembered using the old peeler all these years. The lost hours at the sink. It was just habit; I thought that was all there was. But this was a quantum leap technologically. It must be to do with the angle of the blade."

He leaned forward, put his elbows on his knees, shook his head and looked up, maybe in gratitude. "Sometimes, you just get it. What it's all about. How it all works."

Nobody knew how to follow on from that, but someone had to say something. Maybe it was a weird kind of joke or wind-up and there would be a "Fooled you!" moment. But it didn't feel like that. If anything, I'd say it was tense. And no one knew why. It was abstract.

Alec had a go. He said, in an accommodating tone, "Aye, small things can make a big difference." In the absence of the slightest clue as to what we were even talking about, where we were or where we were going, I thought this was a pretty safe effort. But Collie-Dog looked offended. Hurt, even. He pushed his glasses up his nose and, with a faint crack in his voice, said, "Well. Depends on what you call a small thing."

I can't say we were dumbfounded. Too strong. More like… lost. The conventional conversational cues were gone. There were no signposts. The last response suggested that this was a more sensitive subject than could objectively appear possible. It had become a weird kind of minefield. It didn't even seem right to try to change the subject. Not that anyone knew how to. It was like a spell had been cast over the table.

I tried a different tack: "What did Christine think of the… er… new potato-peeler?" I couldn't believe I was actually saying this.

"She doesn't get it," he said. "Christine has a different perspective. You know women. It's created a bit of a rift, to tell the truth. We'd always got on. Covered for each other. Now she complains whenever we have spuds. Like she's using that to get at me or make a point about the house. Or something. It's not the way it was. It's not comfortable. It's not reasonable."

He looked round, perhaps hoping for some bloke-ish solidarity.

"Does she not like spuds, then?" said Alec a bit desperately. Still trying.

"Even if she didn't," said the Dog, "I was varying it. Mash, chips, roast, sautéed, even plain boiled. Guys" – and here he stopped and looked round the table as if he was making a closing argument to a jury – "the POTATO is the most versatile vegetable out there."

"I never thought of it as a vegetable," said Billy Stripe, "but, yeah, you're right."

Jon E went, "Yeah, like, is a tomato a fruit? I can never remember. And who decides these things anyway?"

Trying to find a foothold, Cream Soda said gamely, "I had a wee hand drill that I used for years. Then I lost it. Left it on a job in a house somewhere. I tried to get the same kind but they'd stopped making them. Bought the new so-called improved model, but it was never as good as the old one."

Good effort. This empathetic approach seemed to loosen things up a bit. For us, anyway. Gave us a bit of direction. Alec chipped in about a pair of boots he'd had once that he wore for years. He could never find the same kind again, so now when he sees something he likes – shoes, T-shirts, whatever – he'll always buy three or four. "I call it defensive retail," he said.

"Aye," John E said, "got you. If it's a big game, I'll always bet on the other team, just so that if we lose, I'll have a wee financial score to soften the blow. If we win, I'm happy anyway. Insurance against disappointment. It's a win-win. Good system."

Not to be out-done, Billy Stripe said, "Me and Marion were away in Inverness without the kids for a couple of days. Went for a pizza at lunchtime. So I had a couple of pints with my pepperoni, before she headed off to M&S. Wandered about for a while, went through the arcade, and then I really needed to pee. Saw this public facility and it was fifty pence. For a slash! No way. So I went back to the pizza place and, as I'm walking to the bogs, this waiter comes over and says to me, excuse me sir, paying customers only. I said, no, *you* excuse me: I'm here on account of the fluids I purchased recently in this establishment. You need to think of it as recycling. Should have seen the look on his face."

Everyone had a laugh. Everyone but the Collie-Dog. I could see he wasn't having it. Either that or he didn't get it. He was, if anything, more agitated. He said, "No, you don't understand. It's not the same thing. None of that." Kind of abrupt. Emphatic, anyway.

Then I heard someone else speak. And, to my surprise, it was me. And I listened to myself talk about that time in Glasgow when I saw a crashed ambulance. "And I thought that if the next one came along and that crashed... and the next one and the next one... and if it carried on all day. And all week. An endless pile-up. Like it was ambulances all the way, forever. Turtles, all the way down. And that's it... really... like, that's like, what it's like. You know. Life."

Jon E said, "Hey, what if it was hearses? There would be no one to bury anyone anymore. It would all just pile up. Forever. Till there was no one left to build them or drive them."

"Good point," I said, "I hadn't thought of that."

And there was a nodding of heads. Probably out of politeness. I felt I'd said something, but – honestly – I wasn't sure what. And neither were they.

It kind of shut everybody up, anyway. For a bit. Until Cream Soda said, "Yeah, remember after Blunder broke his leg? He was sitting on the sofa one day watching TV, in plaster, when the doorbell went. And when he stood up to get his crutches, he fell and broke his arm. Man oh man, he was like that guy who moved from Hiroshima to Nagasaki after surviving the bomb."

Everyone started to laugh again but somehow stopped themselves this time. Jon E asked, in all seriousness, "Who was at the door? Did he manage to let them in?"

Sometimes I wonder about the company I keep.

So, now, nobody knew what to say. Where to go from here? Wherever here was. All routes were closed off. What else was there? We had to wait for the Dog to speak. Who said, "See the weather forecast on the TV, with the satellite pictures of weather systems and clouds and all that? You can see the rain coming over the islands and the whole country, can't you?"

We agreed that this was true. What else were we going to say? Christ alone knew what was coming next.

"And where does the rain come from?" he asked. Maybe rhetorically, but it felt like a leading question. Did he think we were kids? Maybe he felt he was educating us. "Every day's a school day." But, by now, none of us were any the wiser, so – might as well – I said, "Yeah, well, it comes from the sky. It's from the evaporation of the sea and it condenses as rain over the land."

He nodded. "Right." And then, with eyes ablaze, he said, "And does it only fall on the land?" Silence. "No," he said, "it falls on the sea, too. Where it originally came from. Are the rainclouds the exact same shape as the islands and the countries and continents that they come over? A perfect fit? An Isle of Lewis-shaped cloud? A Shetland-shaped cloud. A north of Scotland-shaped cloud?"

"Clouds can look like mashed potatoes, though?" said Alec. Trying to humour him. All over the place. A bit desperate, to be honest. Everyone ignored him.

"No, course they're not," said Cream Soda hopelessly. Trying to recover the situation.

"No. Exactly," said the Dog. Calmly, evenly. In control. "It comes from the sea but it falls on the sea *as well* as on the land."

We waited. Nobody said anything. He looked round at us.

"What's the point of that?" he said.

Part IV

Leftovers

Iain and Coinneach on top of Mùirneag, 1973.

Blank Christmas

We were never big on presents in our house. We got birthday and Christmas gifts from our parents but never gave each other any. Or got or gave any to relatives or neighbours. We weren't mean, unusual or different. It was normal for the time. Later though, with work, girlfriends and their extended families, changing social mores, present giving was unavoidable and became the way things were done. At work, after Christmas there would be the inevitable questions on "what you got". The little rituals. The social conversation.

My mother was by now becoming increasingly scatty. There's a phrase in Gaelic: *ga do chall fhèin*, which means, "losing yourself". And by that Christmas she was lost. To herself and to us. I wasn't in a relationship. Single. Adrift again.

And that was the Christmas that I did not receive a single present. It didn't bother me but I could not admit it at work because that would have been embarrassing. Not for me, for them. So I swathed it in vagueness. Oh, usual things, nothing special … a scarf, socks.

The Lost Shoe

Lunchtime in school and Uisdean and I are walking along the quay. There is a lump of coal, which I kick as hard as I can into the harbour. Lace-less, gusseted slip-ons were the fashion, and while the coal skitters along the quayside – missing an open goal, so to speak – my shoe goes flying off, spinning in a high arc into the sea. It floats briefly before nose-diving, submarine-like below the surface. For a violent second, I have to resist the impulse to leap, to take on the ten-foot drop into the harbour to retrieve it.

The very moment this course of action flares up is the same instant that it is extinguished. There is no solution. Just the situation. I burst into tears.

Out of a Clear Blue Sky

It was a cold, sharp, sunny day and five of us were walking back to school along James Street in Stornoway. I was chewing gum, someone was smoking a fag, and we were gabbing inconsequentially. A most ordinary day. One that only exists, enabled in my memory, because of a *thing that happened*.

A thing that cracked open (to me) the hitherto unknown philosophical space between reality and realisation.

For, as I walked, the *thing that happened* was that my hair became instantaneously slick, warm-wet, drenched, and I was overcome by a foul, nauseating, asphyxiating stench of rotten fish, while – impossibly, as we were on a wide pavement away from any building – a can of white paint had been poured over me and was glooping down the shoulders of my blazer and the back of my neck.

All around, a spontaneous eruption of spluttering hilarity.

It's that brief glimpse of time I can evoke at will, you see. And still wonder at the vast volume of bewilderment contained inside such a very small space. The vacuum of ignorance and complacency before awareness, consciousness, floods in. And I realise that I have been shat upon, copiously, by a large incontinent seagull.

The Happy Smile Club

I was in Primary Six and left class to take my turn in the dental caravan parked in the playground. I sat in the chair, straitjacketed with fear and apprehension, while the dentist clattered his mouth-mirror and metal probe against my teeth, reciting a litany of strange words to the nurse. The only one I remember is "cavity X". Nothing was explained. No reassurances given.

With a hypodermic he sucked the liquid out of a little bottle and – open wide – stuck the long needle into the back of my jaw, under my back tooth on the right. I was given a few minutes to allow the anaesthetic to take effect before he took his pliers and began to pull on my back molar. But it would not come. Still he pulled and still it remained anchored, as rooted as an oak tree. Soon he had his knee on my chest for maximum leverage and traction until, eventually, as I braced and strained to try and keep my head attached to my body, swathed in a nimbus of numbness, I began to hear a loud tearing sound. And then a final wrench and release. In my jaw was a deep red hole.

In the pliers was the tooth, about an inch long, dripping blood.

It grew again. But I kept its predecessor in a jar on my bedroom window for years, like a trophy.

Magic Bus

It was bad enough that we travelled on a bus all the way from Glasgow to our holiday in Blanes on the Costa Brava. Two days there and two days back. What made the return journey twice as long was that the driver had Neil Diamond's *Greatest Hits* on loop. 'Cracklin' Rosie', 'Sweet Caroline', 'I Am… I Said', and all the others. Through Spain, the length of France and England, and into Buchanan Street station in Glasgow.

Rude Awakening

We had been reliably informed that we could have a small house in Calbost in South Lochs over a summer weekend. We arrived Friday and I spent all Saturday fishing; got a good haul of trout, which made a splendid dinner that evening. Sunday, we took our time, and we'd think about heading back on Tuesday. A proper long weekend. About six o'clock on Monday morning there was a thumping at the back door. I dragged myself out of bed, opened it and there was an angry guy standing there who said, "Who are you? We've got this place booked." His family in a Range Rover behind him.

Green for Go

I was project manager on the multi-million-pound development of a new arts centre in Stornoway. It began well enough but pretty soon it blotted the sun from the sky. Obliterated all cheer from my life. The costs rose. The pressure increased. The pressure became stress. The stress became corrosive. It ate me up. One morning, cycling into work, I came to some roadworks with a human traffic light operating the single file system. He had a big red sign that said, "STOP". Which he flipped to green for GO on the reverse side. He did that all day long. I vividly remember thinking, "God, I would absolutely LOVE that job."

Venezia

We queue interminably in the blistering sun for our Biennale tickets. It is thirty-eight degrees. As we inch along, flunkies distribute bottled water. Inside, hours later, a scene of unmitigated chaos. A tower of babble. Had everyone been shouting "rhubarb" in thirteen different languages, it would have made more sense. We get our passes but I'll never understand how. Random distribution to survivors, perhaps.

Early afternoon, a thunderous deluge dries up in a couple of minutes on the frying-pan pavements. Later, to the Scottish Pavilion, panting in the heat, the city now a sauna. Inside, a pale, gingery Scottish curator flushed pink, his cream linen suit a camouflage pattern of dark sweat blots: underarm, crotch and back.

We haven't eaten since breakfast and take a *vaporetta* from the Grand Canal to the restaurant near our hotel on the Lido. Only when aboard do we realise that it is going the wrong way, the long way round: twenty-one stops, not the planned four. Hunger ruins the experience. And we feel guilty about under-appreciating this magical tour of the Grand Canal as the lights begin to wink on in the *palazzi*. Like when a favourite film comes on just when you're ready for bed. You stay up but you wish it was over.

It's dark when we arrive at the Lido. Darker still when there is a power cut. In the blackout, outside the restaurant, the *maître d'* is shouting, "*Tutto Venezia.*" Waving his arms. Guests filing out. Our hotel room now an oven. A sweat-lodge. We crash out, famished, ravenous, with the emergency lighting on. At 3am, the main lights and aircon slam on. Shocking us awake.

Bilge

Before the bridge, Skye was connected to the mainland by the car ferry that ran the short route between Kyle and Kyleakin. Each year, it was taken to the slipway on Goat Island in Stornoway for a refit by Joe Fleming Engineering. Usually in the winter months. I got a job there as a labourer.

Before engine work and painting, there was the clean-up. I was sent down the metal ladder with a light bulb on an extension and a container cut from the bottom half of a plastic carton. My task was to scoop up the gallons of black, black oil in the ship's bilges, take it up the ladder and pour it pint by pint into an oil drum on deck. I had to wear wellies to wade through it. Once that had been done, a couple of days later, I was given a large box of industrial rags to finish the job.

Landing on My Feet

With the Harris Tweed industry contracting, yet another mill was closing down and had to be demolished. Beforehand, our job was to dismantle the sprinkler system. It covered about an acre and would take a couple of days. The piping was mostly narrow standard gauge, although centrally there were larger pipes, all suspended from the ceiling by slim metal brackets. Our system was to place two wooden trestles supporting heavy planks underneath: Up top, I would be at one end and the second boiler suit at the other. In the middle, one of the fitters would burn the brackets, and when freed we would shoulder the weight, lower the pipes to our feet and then to the floor. It was methodical work, and over the two days we had just about dismantled it all. Only the larger pipes remained. They got progressively heavier until, finally, we stood under a horizontal iron tree trunk hanging from three brackets.

Routinely we shunted the trestles into place, put the planks up, and as I stood in position, I watched the steel fitting at my end burn through and detach. I watched the steel fitting at the far end burn and detach. And braced myself. The entire pipe was now held by a single middle bracket. Which I now watched glow deep orange and then turn white. And then I saw it stretch like chewing gum. And then, in a fraction of an instant, I was standing on the concrete floor, in shock, with the trestles in smithereens around me and my ears ringing, the pipe rolling away while the other two picked themselves up.

No harm done. Job done.

Masterplan

Sixth Year, final year in school, a couple of months in. There was an announcement from the Rector, on the daily Absentee sheet: Any pupils leaving that year who did not know what they were doing afterwards would need to report to his office at 12pm. I was being summoned. Since my future as a marine biologist had been scuppered I was clueless. I didn't fancy anything. English at University? Then what? Teaching? Come on.

There were about half a dozen waiting outside his office. When I got called in he glanced at me and asked briskly what O Levels (Standard Grades) and Highers I had. Noted them down. English, Chemistry, Biology... "What's this? You got a B in O Grade Art?" Yes, I took Art in Fifth Year to fill some spare periods. "Have you thought about going to Art School?" No. But you need a Higher for that. "I don't think so. Just a portfolio. Anyway, you're sitting your Higher this year aren't you?" Uh, yes.

He picked up the phone and rang the Art Department. Couple of straight questions. Put the phone down and said "There you have it."

And in that five minutes, although I didn't know it, the rest of my life was mapped out.

On the Same Page

The harbourmaster was Captain Mackay, from Harris. White hair, black eyebrows, brass buttons, brocaded cap, uniform. He smoked a pipe and reeked of deep-sea merchant fleet history. Not a great listener but a good shouter. Most of what he said sounded like an order.

One day, he picked up me and Uisdean in a van to help him with a load. We drove past the open, grassy forecourt on North Beach that was used for drying nets, where the Pier and Harbour Commission had just built a terrace of "equipment stores" for fishermen. As a result, a high rough-casted wall now blocked out the agreeable view across the inner harbour to the Castle Grounds from the Royal Hotel and other properties. It loomed over pedestrians. There were protests, angry letters to the *Stornoway Gazette*. Some wag had spray-painted "Wall Street" across the façade.

The captain began muttering about the equipment stores and the wall as he drove past, and we nodded and agreed with him vociferously that it was an absolute disgrace.

He wasn't listening of course, and went on to pronounce emphatically that it was absolutely essential. Whereupon we agreed with him wholeheartedly. That it was, indeed, necessary and vital. And that nothing could be done. And shook our heads that anyone could think otherwise.

Decades later, the whole edifice was demolished.

On the Slopes

While in Aberdeen I was persuaded by my friend Kenny to come on a college skiing weekend in the Cairngorms. I'd never tried it before – neither had he – but it looked straightforward enough on TV. Didn't have skis but we could hire them. My duffle coat would do for the slopes. Good to go.

Friday, we got the bus to Aviemore, the so-called resort, arrived early evening and checked in at the chalet. To my dismay, we were then sucked out by the peer-tide to a disco located in some GLF (Godforsaken Leisure Facility). It was packed with hard, off-duty squaddies, who were dancing aggressively, ostentatiously, gym-nastically under the light-shower of the glitterball. If you've seen footage of the heyday of Northern Soul at Wigan, you've got the picture.

I wasn't going to do any of that, though. Plan was to drink, play possum, run down the clock and go home. But when I looked up, standing in front of me expectantly was a chunky squaddie in his off-duty Oxford bags, a T-shirt stretched across his chest, Queen's Own Highlanders tattoo on his forearm. He was also wearing his "You dancin'?" face.

I'd been taught the etiquette at school socials that it's impolite to refuse, but it didn't cover this situation. Then he squinted, leaned forward and shouted at me over the thudding soundtrack, "Are you a bloke?!" Mouthed, "Fuck's sake," and turned on his heels.

Next day, we got on the minibus and took a funicular to the slopes. It was steep, windy and paralysingly cold. When I put the skis on, I found I couldn't stand up. When I eventually managed that and began moving, gathering speed, I found I couldn't steer. Or stop. Except by falling over. It wasn't active enough to keep me warm and my duffle coat was getting increasingly waterlogged and heavy. My leg was sore. So I decided that doing nothing and being cold was marginally preferable to this hapless polar slapstick. I had my dignity. There was that.

As I shivered miserably by a ski-fence, a girl from our group in a sky-blue puffy jacket plummeted down and swooped to a stop in front of me in a plume of icy spray, her cheeks pink, her breath a cumulus halo. Phosphorescent, radiant, glowing with heat and energy.

Uphill

I was on the Isle of Barra setting up an exhibition in Castlebay School. It didn't take long and I had the rest of a glorious sun-struck May Day to myself. I decided to climb Eaval, the highest point on the island, which was in easy reach. On the way up, I stopped at the Our Lady Star of the Sea marble sculpture before continuing to the top and following a ridge.

It was a huge, blue day. Spring still carried a residual chill of winter and the air was a crystal prism. Visibility seemed endless. The Outer Hebrides archipelago stretched up through Eriskay and the Uists to Lewis & Harris. The mountains of the Scottish mainland still had some snow on the peaks. I could sense the curvature of the Earth. Felt in touch with the sublime. I could barely comprehend the vastness of the Atlantic but it wasn't necessary to understand. Only to appreciate. To be.

The soundtrack in a film would have been choral, classical, symphonic, harmonic, epic and glorious. A Gaelic psalm or a grand *pibroch*. But in my head was a piece of music that I could not erase or eject and over which I had no control: *Ernie (The Fastest Milkman in the West)*, by Benny Hill. It would not shut up or go away. It seemed to me that I was a vessel stuffed with rubbish, which I had to carry with me everywhere I went. I needed a mental enema.

Bless the Weather

I worked twelve-hour shifts, seven days a week for several months in Stornoway power station, helping build a diesel engine. It was ear-damagingly noisy and tropically hot. You wore ear-protectors all day and the temperature was consistently in the eighties. It didn't matter whether it was a summer's day or the bleak midwinter.

The only evidence of the outside world was a small doorway at the end. Even then, only if it was snowing was there any clue as to what was going on outside. But in the staffroom at tea breaks and lunchbreaks, where there was a large window on the world, our main topic of conversation every day was – inevitably – the weather. "A good day for drying peats." "There's the rain on again."

The King is Dead

In summer 1977, we had a full month travelling round Europe on Interrail, sustained by beer, ice cream and cheese baguettes. Mostly we slept on overnight trains, woke up to a new city, spent the day there and took the last train to the next city or town.

Belgrade, in then Yugoslavia, was the most easterly extreme. Every café, bar, shop, cinema had a portrait of Marshal Tito. Every young man seemed to be in uniform.

Cádiz was the most westerly point, where, sun-scorched and anaesthetised by pints of cheap wine, we slept on the beach. In between, we went to the two-day music festival at the Mont-de-Marsan bullring in France, subsequently dubbed the "Punk Woodstock".

Finally, an overnight ferry from Calais and an early-morning train to London. Up the aisle towards us lurched a strangely familiar but displaced figure – Alex "Hurricane" Higgins, the snooker player. When we got into Victoria the news-stands were emblazoned with *The King is Dead*. It is the 17th of August, 1977. Elvis has left the planet.

We had breakfast in a nearby greasy spoon. In a booth on his own, a Brylcreemed rocker sat with a huge pile of newspapers, silently, sombrely leafing through each and every title published that day.

Gob

Same year, I went to the Marquee in Soho to see The Cortinas. One of the earliest punk bands. It was as though an insane energy had exploded inside this small venue, like a can of beer you've opened after dropping it on a cement floor.

Most shocking was not the outlandish, aggressive styling – studded dog-collars, leather, bin-liners, piercings, spiked hair – or the thrashing music and demented pogoing. It was the spitting. An incessant rain of gob arcing whitely in the spotlights. It ran down the singer's face and dribbled off his nose and chin. It was, in the protocol of the time, a gesture of solidarity and respect. So much respect, he was drenched in it.

Some say that popular music has become over-sanitised. Then, it was savage, raw, primitive and, it has to be said, unhygienic.

Change

Peter's dad had loaned me three hundred and ninety-five pounds to buy a twelve-string Rickenbacker in McCormack's Music. So, as a student, I worked a full summer in a Mac's Imperial bar in Stornoway to be able to pay him back.

The manager was always first in and when I arrived at about 10am he would be sitting on a stool at the bar with his first brandy and port of the day. I could count on the fingers of one hand the number of brandies I sold that summer, yet the bottle on the optic was replaced every couple of days. One night at closing time, he woke after falling asleep at the bar and asked me what time it was. When I said it was quarter past eleven he looked at me in shock, said, "Oh Jesus," and ran and flung the outside doors open. He thought it was morning.

It was the heyday of the oil industry at Arnish Point, where the Drillmaster rig was being constructed. Big money, big guys, big rounds, big sessions. Both before and after work. There were no female toilets. Till systems were rudimentary and the price of rounds was calculated mentally. I became adept at doing it on the hoof: the price of four Te Bheag whiskies, three pints of heavy, two lager, a rum and a double vodka and lemonade. And an orange juice (just kidding).

There was always a squad in from five until they clocked onto the night shift at eight. I took the money and gave the change. "Hey, wait a minute, son," says one. "He gave you a twenty-quid note. You only gave him a fiver back." "No," I say, "I gave him two fivers." The guy in question looks and there's only a fiver in his hand. I go to the till and check. Nope. I return to the bar. There's about a dozen of them now, silent, focused, glaring at me. "Think you can pull a fast one on us, you fly wee bastard?" I don't know what to do. In desperation, I blurt out, "Maybe it's on the floor? Maybe you dropped it?"

He looks down and picks up the missing fiver and continues talking to his mates. No apology necessary.

Magic Touch

The fountainhead of rock 'n' roll, the source, Chuck Berry, was coming to Glasgow. To Tiffany's disco on Sauchiehall Street.

Famous for sure, but also infamously mean and cynical. With good reason, given the racial America he grew up in. He never toured with a band because even if he visited Uzbekistan, there would be a band on hand who knew all his numbers back-to-front. *Johnnie B Goode, Roll Over Beethoven, Sweet Little Sixteen, Back in the USA, Memphis Tennessee...* Ready, willing and able to play for nothing but the privilege of sharing a stage with him.

The greatest tragedy for me was not that he had been banged up for transporting a fourteen-year-old white girl across the border, but that his only number-one record wasn't any of these classics, but the execrable *My Ding-a-Ling*.

Anyway, I didn't go. But later that night I was walking down Renfrew Street from the art school when I saw the back door to Tiffany's was open. So I crept down the steps for a look. Chuck Berry had just finished his set and was negotiating his way through a swarm of fans off-stage. It was a scrum. At its core, this older, slender, Brylcreemed black man in a red, stripy, glittery shirt. I thrust myself in and towards him and actually managed to put my palm on his sweaty back. Like touching the Monolith in *2001*, it would accelerate me to the next stage of my evolutionary development.

Maybe it did help. Because, as I went back up the steps, I heard running and saw a massive bouncer coming for me, and he wasn't giving up. I accelerated down the street for the best part of a mile. Drug-assisted. A massive dose of pure adrenalin.

A Toast

The first time I tried champagne was in the lounge bar of the Seafield Arms Hotel in Cullen, after a day's rehearsal during the shooting of *Local Hero*. I was a natural. Took to it right away and, after the others in our crew had left, Peter and I decided to get another bottle. By then, the only people left in the bar were two senior gents in blazers and ties. The hotel was properly old-school Scottish. It had tartan carpets and an elderly, silver-haired barmaid in pearls and a tartan maxi-skirt. The Queen had stayed there one time.

When our bottle arrived we couldn't open it and, seeing our rather gormless struggle, one of the gents came over and offered his assistance. "I'm usually rather good at this sort of thing," he said. And sure enough, with comparatively little effort, he popped the cork. Grateful, we asked if he and his companion would join us for a drink. He thanked us courteously but declined and returned to his seat.

We were on our second glass when we noticed that the barmaid had gone out. She now returned through the hotel lobby, carrying a silver tray with a half-bottle of champagne and three flutes, and joined the two gentlemen at their table. Odd. Fifteen minutes earlier, they had declined our offer; now they were buying their own.

Bemused, we looked across the bar as they opened their bottle and filled the three glasses with effervescence. And then, in unison, all stood up, raised them aloft and proclaimed, "The Prince. THE PRINCE!"

The date is the 21st of June, 1982. Prince William has just been born.

Inner Space

Morning, on the fifth floor of the Hotel Cosmos in Moscow: I run ahead to catch one of the two lifts just before the doors close. As I bound in, they close behind me and I am immersed in utter, unadulterated, impenetrable, centre-of-the-Earth darkness. Pure. Uncontaminated by the faintest light. And silence. An absolute state. Surrounded by nothingness. Sensory destitution. Only gravity gives me a sense of being upright.

I wait. Nothing happens. More nothing. Nothing intensifies to nothingness. In it, my consciousness drifts untethered. The fading memory of light remains to define the darkness. But it is already becoming a singularity. The lights will come on. Return. But how long? Did the lift move? Will I know if it does? Will they come and find me?

I reach to feel for the walls. Do something. DO something. I feel my way round the sides until I find the doors and trace the seam down the middle where they meet. I pull them apart. Light smashes in and I step out onto the fifth floor, where I stepped in... how long ago? I don't know. I'm shaking.

Perestroika

In 1989 in Leningrad, as it was then, I bought a souvenir Swatch. It had a red dial with a yellow Soviet hammer-and-sickle symbol at twelve o'clock. Round the watch face, clockwise, the other eleven numbers spelled out P-E-R-E-S-T-R-O-I-K-A: Mikhail Gorbachev's signature 'restructuring' policy as he drew back the iron curtain and began to engage with the West.

Back home, on the morning of the 20th August 1991, my radio alarm woke me to the alarming news on the *Today* programme of a military coup in Russia. Gorbachev and his family were under house arrest at their holiday dacha on the Black Sea. I got up and noticed that, overnight, the watch had stopped.

Worse than Useless

My friend Stephen was a golfer. Not serious but decent, useful. Had a knack. My problem with golf wasn't the game, it was – with the exception of John Updike - golfers. With their stupid checks, Pringle jumpers, clubbiness, conservatism, entitlement and attitude.

One night in the pub, challenged by Stephen, I took up the gauntlet. I would play golf and presumably recant and join the club. At seven o'clock next morning in the pitch dark, I crossed Glasgow to his house, from where we headed out of town to a public golf course. I had assumed there would be some privacy where I could practice, figure it out and get into the swing of it, so to speak. Not so, we had to join a queue and, for the first time in my life, I held a golf club and stood at a tee with a long line behind me, critically checking out my stance and impatiently waiting to get on.

I took aim and lashed the empty air. It took about six swings to hit the ball. When I did, it fell off the tee and trickled a few feet forward. A couple of crusty old bastards came up to Stephen and said, "That boy shouldnae be on a golf course. Saturday is for serious golfers."

It didn't help that I didn't want to be there. The day was a quintessence of frustration and humiliation, and I resolved never to take up a club again. Until, in Skye, a couple of years later when, not unreasonably, I deduced that it would be impossible to be any worse. I was wrong. Again I swung viciously into vacancy until I finally made contact. The ball went backwards. Ended up behind me.

The Heat of the Night

We were on holiday in Andalucía. The four of us hired a car in Malaga, spent a week in Granada, a night in Cordoba and, late one suffocating afternoon, drove into Seville. Famously, the warmest city in Europe. Round and round we went, looking for a place to stay until, eventually, we found some sort of apartment.

Alasdair got the room with air conditioning, Stephen and Anne a double room (without air-con), and I was led up, outside, to a concrete box on the roof. My bunker. It had no windows and was only big enough for a single bed. I could just about stand up in it.

That night, I might as well have been a loaf of bread in an oven, or a clay pot in a kiln. The entire building below me, having absorbed the baking heat of the day like a giant storage heater, slowly, mercilessly released it up through the floor. The following morning, desiccated as a raisin, I creaked down the stairs to prepare to enter the furnace of the coming day.

Freddie Mercury

Early Christmas afternoon, 1991, my uncle pulled up outside our house. He was taking us for a family Christmas dinner at one of the Stornoway hotels. I got in the passenger seat and waited for my mother and two other brothers to come out, when, apropos of nothing, staring straight ahead, my uncle declared, "Freddie Mercury." I looked at him. "Hello" or "Merry Christmas" would have been a more conventional conversational gambit. Best not to ask. "He died," he continued. "I know," I said. "That's right. Of course you know. Freddie Mercury died. No more Freddie. Freddie no more. It was on the front page of every newspaper in the country. It was on the national news, all over the television and the radio. It was all anybody talked about."

He paused, still staring straight ahead, now nodding, and said, "I never heard of him."

Anthropomorphism

We were having dinner after an exhibition opening by the Russian art collective Sharmanka, who had premiered their latest, fabulous machine construction in our gallery. It was adorned with symbolic, carved wooden animals – monkeys, bears, mice – performing an intricate, clever choreography to music.

Making conversation, Moira asked, "If we were animals, what do you think we would be?" Instantly, Tatyana replied, "Moira, she is lioness!" Further down the table, Douglas was afforded arctic fox status. Yes, I could see that was a good fit.

Me? I was a harder match and she conferred intently with her husband, Eduard, for a few minutes before declaring triumphantly, "Rrroddy. He is... a stoat!"

Emergency

I was walking in to work and, while passing one of the grand houses on Goathill Crescent, became aware of a very elderly lady in a tweed skirt and cardigan waving and beckoning me from between the arched portico of her porch. I paused and looked around to check that it actually *was* me she wanted. There was no one else. *Come, come,* she seemed to be saying, *come.* Waving her arm.

So I opened the gate, walked cautiously up the rose-bordered path and, as I approached, she turned into the house, all the while gesticulating: *come, come.* She didn't – perhaps couldn't – speak. Through the house. *Follow me. Come.* I was, by now, braced for the worst. A husband dead of a stroke or heart attack. Something like that. We went down the hall and through into the kitchen, where she handed me a jar of beetroot. I said, "You want me to open it?" She nodded silently, urgently. *Yes. Yes, yes.* So I twisted the lid off, handed it back to her and left.

Melancholy

Bearded, bear-like, bluff, Allan Gray was a cabinet-maker who had moved from the Bristol area to an old croft house in Carloway on the west side of Lewis. His workshop, recreated in the outbuildings, was akin to an artisan laboratory, wall-racked on three sides with dozens of esoteric woodcarving tools redolent of surgery or dentistry. Each one looked like it was in regular use too: keen, oiled, polished, glinting. There were vices, G-clamps, planes, mallets and gauges in immaculate order on a heavy workbench.

He made a bit on the side as a picture-framer and, on account of the guaranteed excellence of his workmanship, I went over with a number of artworks to be re-framed. Among them a sublime, evocative etching by Will Maclean RSA. A dark, laden sky oppresses a West Highland landscape while in the distance, heading out of a sea loch, is the emigrant ship. In the foreground, a dark totem composed of symbols of ruin: a wooden boat, its back and planking broken, filled with stones from an evicted croft – a coffin, sacks, sheep skull, domestic utensils, fishing gear and a deflated, collapsed sail. Above it, rising to the sky, blowing out to sea, a grainy plume of black smoke from the burning thatch.

It's a sombre, stark image of the Clearances, in ambience reminiscent of de Chirico's empty, haunted landscapes.

As we discussed the job, all attempts at small talk failed. Petered out. He was impervious to humour. Gentle jokes flew past him. Conversational gambits were refuted. Each exploratory, connective path led to a dead end. He wasn't unfriendly or intimidating; he just assessed the job and posed a lot of questions, mostly technical, on specifications, measurements, materials, requirements. He also noted down the titles of each work with a pencil. "What's this one called?" he said, looking solemnly at the Will Maclean.

I said, "That one is called *The Melancholy of Departure*."

He looked at me, roared with laughter and shook his head. It was a couple of minutes before he was able to compose himself.

Evolution

It's 1967. I'm ten. Iain, Coinneach and I are planning yet another Saturday fishing expedition, this time to Loch Ullabhat. We've never been.

But our endlessly helpful neighbour, old Kennag Ruadh, warns us forebodingly that we mustn't go. That it's a deep, dark loch and there's a creature in it. An *uilebheist*. The word even sounds like the name of the loch. People have seen it and run away. Escaped.

It's convincing and alarming but if it's meant to put us off, it fails. In fact, it's a further incentive. Now we are definitely going.

Until we learn that on that same day, *One Million Years BC* is coming to the Picture House in Stornoway. A film about dinosaurs. Also featuring – prominently – Raquel Welch. A human intervention that somewhat spoils it for me because it's so unrealistic. Having studied the subject avidly, I know that by the time humans arrive on Earth, dinosaurs have long been extinct. I have books, stickers and a small collection of fossils, including a prehistoric shark's tooth.

It's a dilemma and we debate what to do. The defining issue is monsters. And we reason that if we go to the loch we *might* see one, but if we go to the film it's *guaranteed*. So we go to the film.

And there they are: pterodactyls, a brontosaurus, triceratops, an allosaurus, in a fight to the death. A colossal turtle crests a sand dune like one of Rommel's tanks and Raquel shouts "Archelon", which I recognise as the name of that species from the Cretaceous period. I'm impressed she knows that.

But more unsettling and memorable than the giant reptiles is the tactile frisson elicited by her vestigial fur bikini, veiling and caressing the golden flesh of thigh, breast and … and the glossy

246

blonde hair, and the long sea-dewed limbs of the other female Shell People, lingerie-ed in animal skin, as they frolic in the surf, harpooning fish.

It's compulsive, compelling yet incomprehensible. This irrelevant stuff and fluff isn't what I came to see. But it keeps coming back to me. Unsummoned. Incessant. A flashback on loop. Why? And why does it make me feel so ... so confused?

Sculpture from the Id

After art school I submitted a wood carving to a local exhibition. It was of a bird with a long neck curling in on itself. I was told by someone I respected that it was "well resolved, accomplished. Sensual." In fact, he described it as "overtly sexual". I might have commented that this was incidental. Unintentional. I saw it more as a lost descendent, of Brâncuși, albeit several times removed.

A few days later, a woman I thought I knew quite well came and asked me about it in a serious, concerned tone of voice. She had been told that it was my work. When I confirmed that this was so, she looked at me in astonishment, disbelief, and said, "I'm so sorry. I had to ask. It's just that I find it impossible to equate or connect that piece to you in any way, shape or form."

Who You (Don't) Know

We were going to host a whimsical exhibition called *The Origins of Golf*, by German artist Reinhard Behrens. Few people know that the game began in the Arctic among the Inuit.

Along with the paintings, I decided to build on the concept with some golfing memorabilia. Someone gave me a name so I phoned up St Andrews and was put through immediately to an agreeable, well-spoken gentleman. We chatted for some time and despite my handicap – ignorance – he was polite, patient and helpful.

A couple of years later when the British Open was at St Andrews, I saw "that's the guy I was talking to" on telly. He was Sir Michael Bonnallack, Secretary of the Royal and Ancient and – arguably – the leading golf administrator on the planet.

It shows how far you can go when you haven't got a clue.

Frozen

My paternal grandfather emigrated to Canada before the Great War but returned to do his duty and subsequently married and stayed in Stornoway. He'd had a farm outside Regina in Saskatchewan, an island in a sea of empty grassland that stretched from horizon to horizon. It was defined by isolation and extreme: scorched in the summer, deep frozen in the winter. His nearest neighbour was ten miles away. The people he had left behind on the Isle of Lewis might as well have been on the moon.

One winter day in Regina, it was in the order of twenty below and he was standing on the sidewalk, waiting for a delivery, when he saw a familiar figure approach. To his astonishment, he recognised him as someone from Stornoway. The man merely glanced at him as he passed and, without breaking stride, said, "Your face is frozen, cove." And carried on.

He had pointed out the growing patch of frostbite on his face.

Hudson's Bay

The Hudson's Bay Company used to advertise in the *Stornoway Gazette* every year, recruiting for workers for their stores in remote Canadian provinces. People who knew all about isolation, solitude, lack of amenities. Livestock. People like us.

After leaving Aberdeen for unemployment and assorted communal drudgery, Uisdean and I both agreed that emigration and a "new life" in Canada was the way to go. So we applied and soon got notification that we would be interviewed – back in Aberdeen. Hector Campbell across the road, a bit younger, had also heard back.

Hungover, we turned up on the morning of the interview in a hotel lobby and, in due course, I was called up to one of the rooms. Inside, sitting on the bed was a bald, sun-browned, walnut-faced, middle-aged man with glasses in a shiny, light-grey suit. I sat in a chair and the interview began. Each of the twenty or so questions, delivered in an indifferent Canadian drawl, had either a yes or no answer, which he ticked off on his clipboard without even looking up. "Do you have a girlfriend?" *No*. Tick. "Do you mind staying with a family of a different religion?" *No*. Tick. "Do you drink?" *Umm, occasionally*... Tick. After rattling through his list, he took out a fat roll of cash and peeled off several tenners for my expenses. Took my word for it. Didn't bother with receipts.

A few weeks later, we heard that we had all been accepted. We were going to Canada. And then the lines went dead. I wrote back asking for an update. Be patient, they said. Over the coming weeks, Uisdean got a job in the bank and pulled out. And then, eventually, I got a letter confirming that I wouldn't be going. Canadian immigration was clamping down; they were only allowing half the intake. It would be the last year Hudson's Bay advertised in Scotland.

Hector went, though – only to write forlorn, desperate letters home. Marooned in a hardware store on some dreary prairie. It transpired that, as a Campbell, he had the misfortune of having been in the first half of the alphabet when they made the cut. I guess winning isn't everything.

If you stuck it out for two years, the company would pay your return fair. I don't know if he did.

Three in a Bed

In Stornoway, I had hosted an evening about Scottish football with Bob Crampsey. A former headmaster and one of the most learned commentators and broadcasters on The Game. A few days later, I was in a Glasgow taxi in the early hours of Sunday morning, heading back to my B&B near Charing Cross. Impossibly, at 3am, a live commentary by Bob Crampsey of that day's Rangers match was on the radio. And I wasn't on drugs. I had to ask, and the driver said that he had recorded the game on cassette to listen to through the night.

The place wasn't up to much. A converted tenement with the original rooms crudely subdivided, partitioned off. My single bed was in a corner, next to a now permanently locked internal door. Exhausted, lights out, I was about to drop off when I became aware of the occupants of the adjacent room coming in because of the light filtering through the door frame. And the brief, urgent conversation. And then their lights went out.

And then the grunting, the pounding, the gasps and the squeals, the trampolining mattress, the ohs… the no-oh-nos… oh… no-don't-stop… please yes, yes-yes, yesyesyes… On and on it went, punctuated by the occasional thunk of head against plasterboard.

Separated only by this thin skin of wall and door, I might as well have been in bed with them. I could almost feel the guy breathing in my ear. It was the closest I've ever come to a three-some. Probably a couple of feet.

Mistaken Identity

On a similar theme. My late friend Robbie Neish often accompanied me when touring exhibitions. At five o'clock on a Sunday morning in January 1987, we set off via Tarbert in Harris, through Skye, heading for the McManus Galleries in Dundee.

It was as cold as I have ever experienced in Scotland. The foreshore at the ferry terminal was icebound. But there wasn't much snow until we hit the mainland and drove down the west coast. Now the roads narrowed and with intermittent and then sustained blizzard conditions, the pace slowed. And slowed. It got dark. In the headlights, a herd of deer sprayed across the road in front of us. The narrowest miss. We made it to Crieff – just – and found an old threadbare hotel, where we got a couple of rooms. Hunker down, see what the morning brings.

Aside from being the only two people in the bar, we were the only residents. An attractive and pleasant young barmaid served us. Other than ordering drinks, we didn't talk to her much, but we certainly talked to each other about her.

Later on, we called it a night and, as I lay in bed, voices intruded into the silent chamber next door. A couple. We were not the only guests, after all. And judging by the unselfconscious, uninhibited, expressive and sustained sound effects, it's likely they thought they were alone, too. The dark vacuum in my head lit up with vivid, animated, sensational imagery. In the bottomless gloom of this gothic pile it was as if rampant, erotic poltergeists had come to haunt me and taunt me. Bumps in the night, you might say.

Next morning, Robbie and I were the only two at breakfast. "Sleep well?" he offered. "All right," I said. "I was pretty tired. You?"

"Not bad, not bad." For no apparent reason, though, he was smiling and looking at me with what might have been admiration. Maybe even respect. "It sounded like you had a good night," he said.

"How do you mean, it *sounded* like I had a good night?"

"You and that wee barmaid. Nice one."

It's a hard thing to confront and admit, but I had a responsibility. Reluctantly, I had to tell him that, alas, things like that didn't happen in real life. Not to me, anyway. That there is no Santa Claus.

Still, I suppose I was somewhat flattered.

Famous Last Words:
Beginning, Middle and End

I was born at home in a downstairs room, in the village of Coll in the Isle of Lewis. After returning from college I continued to live there until I was fifty years of age, when I bought my first house. At fifty-three, I became a father. I worked in the same job for more than thirty-five years and will be buried in the local cemetery at Gress, along with my forebears and everyone else from the district. It's beside the river where I used to fish, and across the road from the beach and the machair where, in my youth, we sometimes drank carry-outs in the car.

Part V

Swan Songs Unsung

Shiant Isles encampment, 1973.

Lyrics

A BOOZE TRILOGY
One
(On drinking too much. Or maybe not enough)

Thirst
Drought that's in my soul
Thirst I can't control

The bills come floating through my door
Fall like confetti to the floor
At a forlorn wedding in the spring
In a one-horse town called Could-a-been

I bit off more than I could chew
I tried to bite the bullet too
I did my best to do my worst
And as a loser I came first

Now I'm off the leash
I'm on the lash
I'm flogging a dead horse too
I'm a busted lush
I can never drink enough
To ever forget about you

The never-ending lost weekends
The useless sympathetic friends
The things I never knew I knew
The things I tried and failed to do

But I'm off the leash
I'm on the lash
I'm walking in iron shoes
I'm a busted lush

Bleak

I can never drink enough
To ever forget about you

I know one drink is one too much
And that an ocean ain't enough
But still that tide runs through my veins
And I'm still anchored to this pain

I'm off the leash
I'm on the lash
I'm swimming in iron shoes
I'm a busted lush
I can never drink enough

To ever forget over you

* * *

Two
(On trying not to drink)

The Long Night
The evening stretches before me
Like the empty open sea
For miles and miles there's nothing there
From the TV to my chair

Echoes fade and disappear
And the hours turn into years
The long, long night goes on and on
And never ever meets the dawn

And there's a bottle in the cupboard but I can't touch that
There's a bottle in the cupboard but I can't touch that
There's a bottle in the cupboard but I can't touch that
But tonight's an emergency
Yes tonight's an emergency
Every night's an emergency

The sky above, the earth below
The future gives me vertigo
The long, long night goes on and on
And I can't forget you're gone

I can't endure these endless minutes
I can't afford the precious time
I always thought that you'd come back here
I always thought you'd change your mind

And there's a bottle in the cupboard but I can't touch that
There's a bottle in the cupboard but I can't touch that
There's a bottle in the cupboard but I can't touch that
But tonight's an emergency
Every night's an emergency

Every night's an eternity

* * *

Three

CHEAP BOOZE: An Incantation

I'm a little acute and I'm a little obtuse
I've been riding on the blunder bus, I got an excuse
I'm a little bit sensitive I easily bruise
I'm in touch with my feelings, I'm in touch with cheap booze

Cheap booze, I'm a free man I can do what I choose
Cheap booze, I'm a prisoner of own views
And I'm relatively comfortable in my brown shoes
I'm a kind of academic and I study cheap booze

Are you a detective, are you looking for clues?
Are you psychedelic or just a little confused?
Ah, what's with all the questions? I don't do interviews
I'm heading for the check-out with a slab of cheap booze

Bleak

So get the party started, go and light the fuse,
Look at all the neighbours with their beers and barbecues
Better slip into your sleeping bag and join the long queues
It's gonna be a long night but we're good for cheap booze

Cheap booze, come and get it, you got nothing to lose
Cheap booze, you don't have to put your head in a noose
You don't need a risk assessment, you don't need to peruse
Any terms and conditions, what you get is cheap booze

Now here come the wombats, here come the kangaroos
They're juggling with boomerangs and didgeridoos
We got bandicoots with parachutes and squawky cockatoos
It's the inevitable consequence of lots of cheap booze

Which gets me thinking about the stuff I overdo and overuse
I'm not an intellectual but I do have strong views
If this was an election, who or what would you choose?
I'm kind of undecided, but I lean to cheap booze.

Because it's a free country, that's the end of the news
Wasn't it dear ole Noel who had a talent to amuse?
Well don't ever underestimate my power to schmooze
I'm an anti-social butterfly high on cheap booze

And I'll serve my life sentence just the way that I choose.

You might think I'm good for nothing but I'm good for cheap booze

* * *

(On what we leave behind)

LONG TIME DEAD
I'll take from here
A souvenir
A memory of my life

Look at all these objects, look at all these things
Trinkets and antiquities and ornaments and rings
Curios and oddities, china figurines
Bric-a-brac and manuscripts, testaments of Kings

All dead, the people who made them
All dead, the people who sold them
All dead, the people who owned them
All dead: you'll be a long time dead

Look at all these relics, earthenware and bones
Heritage and legacy, empty stately homes
Derelict and desolate, gardens overgrown
Debris and detritus, empires overthrown

All dead, the people who built them
All dead, the people who lived there
All dead, the people who left there
All dead: you'll be a long time dead

Now look at all these soldiers, walking in a line
Straddling the border of the living and the dying
Cenotaphs and epitaphs, crypts and mausoleums
Monuments and obelisks, obsolete museums

All dead, the people who went there
All dead, the people who sent them
All dead, the people who lost them
All dead: you'll be a long time dead

Everything is relative, everything you see
Everyone who came before, everyone to be

Gathered in the garden, in the dappled greenery
Generations composting beneath the family trees

All dead, all dead, all dead, all dead
We'll be a long time dead

Still the world remains,
The world remains,
The world remains
Without us

* * *

(On emotional disengagement)

DINNER ON THE BATTLEFIELD

Candlelight glints off the silverware
In a restaurant with antique tableware
The cut and thrust of cutlery
The clash of steel on crockery

Don't you know your history? she said
The past is waiting for you up-ahead,
The friendly fire, the broken truces
The sad parade of lame excuses

Dinner on the battlefield
Trying to be tactical
Dinner on the battlefield
Trying to be tactical

All is fair in love and war, they say,
But will we live to fight another day?
Faded words and wounded roses
The candles die and the evening closes

Dinner on the battlefield

Trying to be tactical

Lyrics

* * *

(On when the ferry is storm-bound and the supermarket shelves
are bare… in the pre-coronavirus world)

THRENODY: STORNOWAY WINTER, 2014

Trudging along on the Tesco trail
Trying to find some holy grail
My head and my heart and my feet are sore
But I keep on pushing the metaphor
Keep on searching, come what may
Keep on trying to make some hay
Feels like I've been this way before
It's almost harder than looking for
The last pint of milk in Stornoway
On a wind-whipped, rain-lashed winter's day.

Peppered by the bulleting hail
In a sinking boat we can never bale
All washed up on the crashing shore
With a brittle mind and a broken oar
The light is draining from the day
Last night I heard the raven say
"Nevermore, nevermore"
It's almost harder than looking for
The last pint of milk in Stornoway
On a wind-whipped, rain-lashed winter's day

The world's made up of guests and hosts
The world is full of wasps and ghosts
Sometimes it feels like being at war
(Nobody knows what that's good for)
Whether you're happy or in despair
Whether you think it's wrong or fair
Take your knocks and pay your share

Bleak

The weather doesn't know or care
It never rains, it only pours
But it doesn't matter anymore
We've all been down this way before
It's getting harder than looking for
The last pint of milk in Stornoway

On a wind-whipped, rain-lashed winter's day

* * *

(On the everyday insanity of parenthood)

BATMAN PANTS
It is what it is and we are where we are
It is what it is and we are where we are
It is what it is and we are where we are
It is what it is and we are where we are

My Batman pants, my Batman pants
I've got ants in my Batman pants
My Batman pants, my Batman pants
Can I be your lucky mascot in my Batman pants?

I need that duck, I need that duck
Daddy Daddy Daddy, I need that duck
I need that duck, I need that duck
Daddy Daddy Daddy, I need that duck

Ah HA HA, that fat elephant
Can't fit into my Batman pants
The rules are skimpy, the rules are scant
They don't apply to my Batman pants
Go to bed! I shan't, I shan't
I'll take away your Batman pants
NO WAY NO WAY, you can't, you can't
Beat the superpower of my Batman pants

Lyrics

It is what it is and we are where we are
It is what it is and we are where we are
It is what it is and we are where we are
It is what it is and we are where we are

Well, there's a baddy hiding in the trees
His teeth are yellow and he smells of cheese
He's got spots on his nose that he needs to squeeze
We'll drop a pepper-bomb to make him sneeze

You can hear him cough, you can hear him wheeze
See him grope and shuffle on his knees
He don't say thanks and he don't say please
He ate the fish and chips but he left the peas

He's got corkscrew hair he combs with grease
The joint is jumping with his fleas
Drop that gun! Get your hands up, freeze!
I'm not gonna let you shoot the breeze

Feed the ducks, feed the ducks,
Fa-Fa, Fa-Fa, Fa-Fa, Fa-Fa, Feed the ducks
Feed that duck, feed that duck,
Fa-Fa, Fa-Fa, Fa-Fa, Fa-Fa Feed that duck
Fava beans, Fava beans,
Fa-Fa, Fa-Fa, Fa-Fa, Fa-Fa Fava beans
Fava beans, Fava beans,
Fa-Fa, Fa-Fa, Fa-Fa, Fa-Fa Fava beans

O my Batman pants, my Batman pants
I'm growing plants in my Batman pants
My Batman pants, my Batman pants
I've got a big eggplant in my Batman pants

I saw what I saw and I did what I did
I heard what I heard and I hid where I hid
I saw what I saw on the saucy see-saw
No I did, no I didn't, no I did, no I didn't

Bleak

No I didn't, no I didn't, no I didn't, no I did. So

My Batman pants, my Batman pants
I got a government grant for my Batman pants
My Batman pants, my Batman pants
Everybody wants my Batman pants
My Batmanbatmanbatmanbatman
batmanbatmanbatmanbatman
PANTS

* * *

(On not trying anymore)

CHEERIO, CHEERIO
No more
No more rage
Raging against the growing of my waist
Recline into my fat armchair
Relax, forget and float
Collapse, unwind and yield
Abstain from abstinence
Leave the field
Mainline the marshmallow
Base-jump the blancmange
Submerge in beige
At rest in a nest in my fluffy cage
A last post for my libido, bow and kneel
Retire this rodent from the wheel
Average out the pull and shove
Embrace the things I hate to love
Take down the bright flag and salute
As the sun goes down on my distant youth

* * *

(Finally, along with useful next-door facilities such as a garage and a plumber, I live down the road from the undertaker. This is an observation on the routine business of mortality in a small community. Written in and for "normal times", it pre-dates Covid-19)

EPITAPH

Hand in hand
Walking the kids to school
On a soft September
In Stornoway
I notice from a lorry
Round the back
A consignment of coffins
Being unloaded:
New stock, merchandise
A routine delivery, nothing more
Ah, but who are they for?
These capsules for our oblivion
These vessels for our cut flowers
Each to be allocated at an anointed hour
Each to contain the extinct content
That will validate its purchase
And complete its purpose
Unknown to us until we notice,
In passing, a familiar name
In the butcher's window.
And, there can never be
An oversupply or surplus,
Because demand is endless
And continuous

Bleak

Through the news-less days
The wallpaper years
The all-purpose plod
And the gentle attrition
Of our modest, miniature,
Apocalypse.

* * *

Things My Mother Used to Say to Us

- What fresh hell is this?
- We have created monsters that rose up to devour us.
- Youth is a wonderful thing; it's a pity it's wasted on the young.
- When you got it, did you want it?
- A cat can look at a King.
- No information given to the enemy.
- The things you see when you haven't got your gun.
- Men have died and worms have eaten them, but not for love.
- Was your journey really necessary?
- He that is down shall fear no fall, he that is low no ill.
- If you were hungry, you would eat it.
- Full many a flower was born to blush unseen and spend its sweetness on the desert air.
- Worse things happen at sea.

Glossary

àirigh – summer sheiling or bothy

braon – drop, dew

bùirseach – deluge

cailleach – old woman

canach – cotton-grass

cèilidh – a social visit. A traditional Scottish gathering with dancing and Gaelic music.

ceòthran – slight drizzle

ceud mìle fàilte – "one hundred thousand welcomes" (saying)

cianalas – homesickness

còinneach – bog, moss

crotal – lichen

cuibhrig – a densely woven, heavy wool blanket

cur na mara - seasickness

cutag – a knife for gutting herring

dìle – flood

dorgh – a handline (for fishing)

drùisealachd – moisture, perspiration

feannagan – raised lazy-beds

fraoch – heather

fuachd – cold

ga do chall fhèin– "losing yourself" (saying)

luachair – rushes

machair – low-lying Hebridean coastal grassland and pasture

mòine – peat, moss, morass

mòinteach bhriste – broken moorland

mùirneag – gentle or civil woman. Also, 'the beloved one'.

Glossary

pìobaireachd (pibroch) – playing on bagpipes; usually refers to a lament

Sasannach – English person (from *Sasainn*; England)

Sgitheanach – person from Skye

Sil – rain, drop, drip

sleipean – slate-pen

smùid – vapour, fine spray

tuil – flood, torrent, deluge

uilebheist – monster, water serpent

uisge mìn – fine rain

A Note on Gaelic

I'm a fluent native Gaelic speaker but not an academic. It's the language I grew up with, when you could tell which village someone came from by their accent. Some of it is local vernacular. I still tend to use the older spellings.

Acknowledgements

Thanks to Moira, always, Alex Boyd for giving me the original motivation to do this (albeit via borderline persecution), An Lanntair for support and sanctuary, Gerry Cambridge for editorial advice, Peter Capaldi for the shared experience and added if incongruous star quality, Steve Dilworth, Finlay Macleod and Stephen Perry who cast a cold eye on the early drafts, Jonathan Meades (the Boswell of Rust), The Munros (Donald John and family, not the mountains) for allowing me to share their misfortune, Jordan Ogg at *The Island Review*, Matthew Dalziel + Louise Scullion, Stornoway Writers' Circle, Dr John Smith, Domhnall Macleod (Tolstadh a' Chaoilis), Laurie Cuffe with apologies for purloining his material. Jane and Mrs Kirsty Maciver, Jon Macleod, John Maclean, Sam Maynard, for photography.

Thanks to my parents, forebears, brothers, aunts and uncles, cousins, friends et al, the characters and personnel who appear in the preceding pages as themselves or in different skins. Anybody I've forgotten who think they should be mentioned (Your Name Here). If you've got this far, thanks for reading.

Special thanks to Sara Hunt at Saraband. Also Craig Hillsley.

Some pieces have appeared in different forms in *The Island Review*, *Northwords Now* and *Beyond Words* (Stories and Poems from the Western Isles).

The publisher is grateful to Peter Capaldi for giving the author permission to quote lyrics that were collaboratively written, such as for the song on page 83, 'Bela Lugosi's Birthday', and for the photograph on page 77 to be reproduced here.

Brown trout from fishing expedition to Loch Mor Eileabhat on North Lewis moor, 1971.